LOCAL STREET ATLAS

THANET CANTERBURY

ASH · BROADSTAIRS · CHARTHAM · EASTRY · HERNE
HERNE BAY · LITTLEBOURNE · MARGATE · MINSTER
RAMSGATE · SANDWICH · WHITSTABLE

CONTENTS

Page Layout & Road Map 2
4 Miles to 1 Inch

Margate Enlarged Centre 3
7 Inches to 1 Mile

Ramsgate Enlarged Centre 4
8 Inches to 1 Mile

Broadstairs Enlarged Centre 5
7 Inches to 1 Mile

Canterbury Enlarged Centre 6
8 Inches to 1 Mile

Street Maps 7-39
4 Inches to 1 Mile

Index to Streets 39

Minor Road
Pedestrianized / Restricted Access
Track
Built Up Area
Footpath
Stream
River
Canal (Lock)
Railway / Station
Post Office
Car Park / Park & Ride
Public Convenience
Place of Worship
One-way Street
Tourist Information Centre
Adjoining Pages
Area Depicting Enlarged Centre
Emergency Services
Industrial Buildings
Leisure Buildings
Education Buildings
Hotels etc.
Retail Buildings
General Buildings
Woodland
Orchard
Recreational / Parkland
Cemetery

www.philips-maps.co.uk

First published in 2004 by
Estate Publications

This edition published by Philip's,
a division of Octopus Publishing Group Ltd
www.octopusbooks.co.uk
2–4 Heron Quays, London E14 4JP
An Hachette Livre UK Company
www.hachettelivre.co.uk

Second edition 2008
02/02-08

ISBN 978-0-540-09383-0

Printed in China by Toppan

PAGE LAYOUT & ROAD MAP

Scale: 4 Miles to 1 Inch

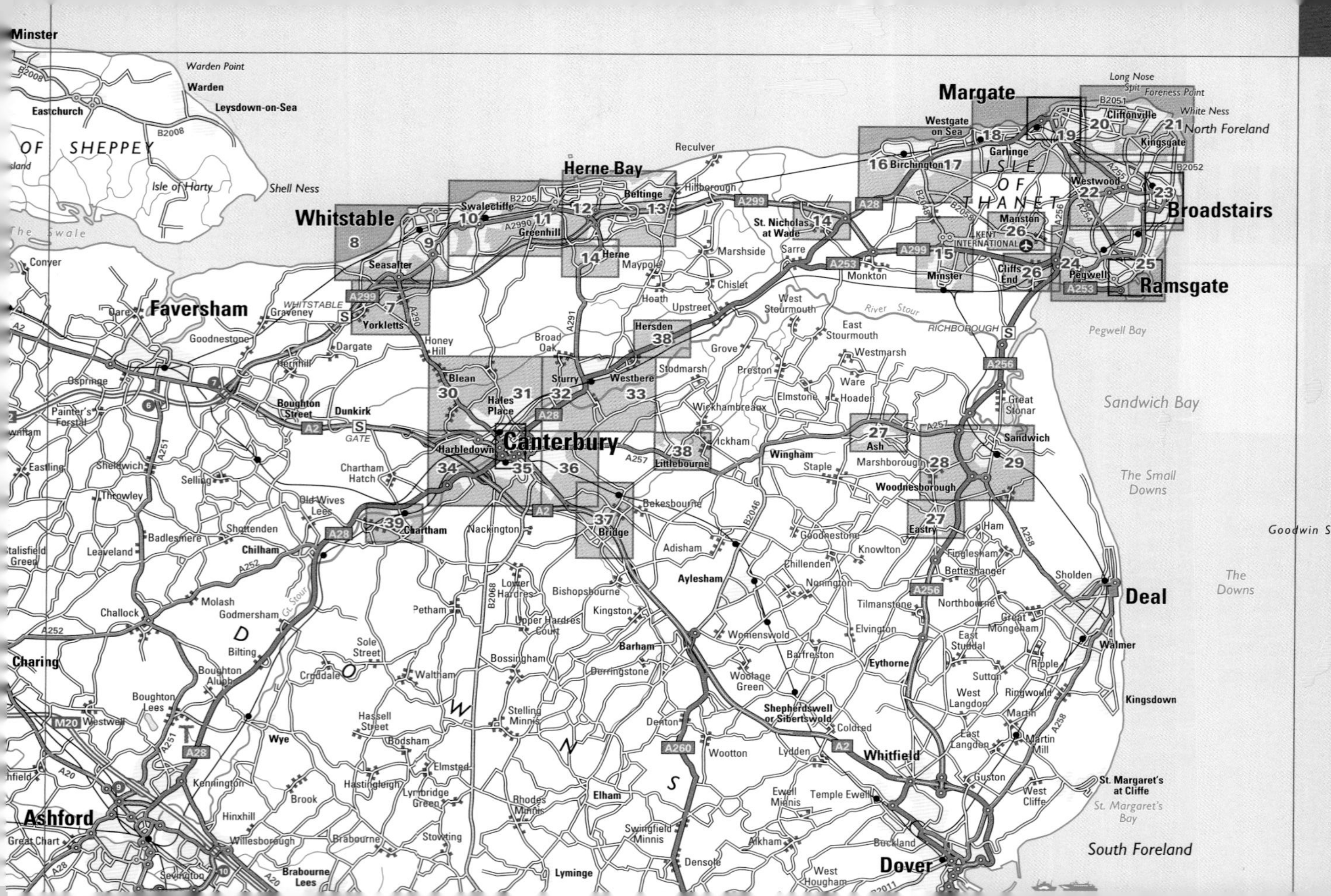

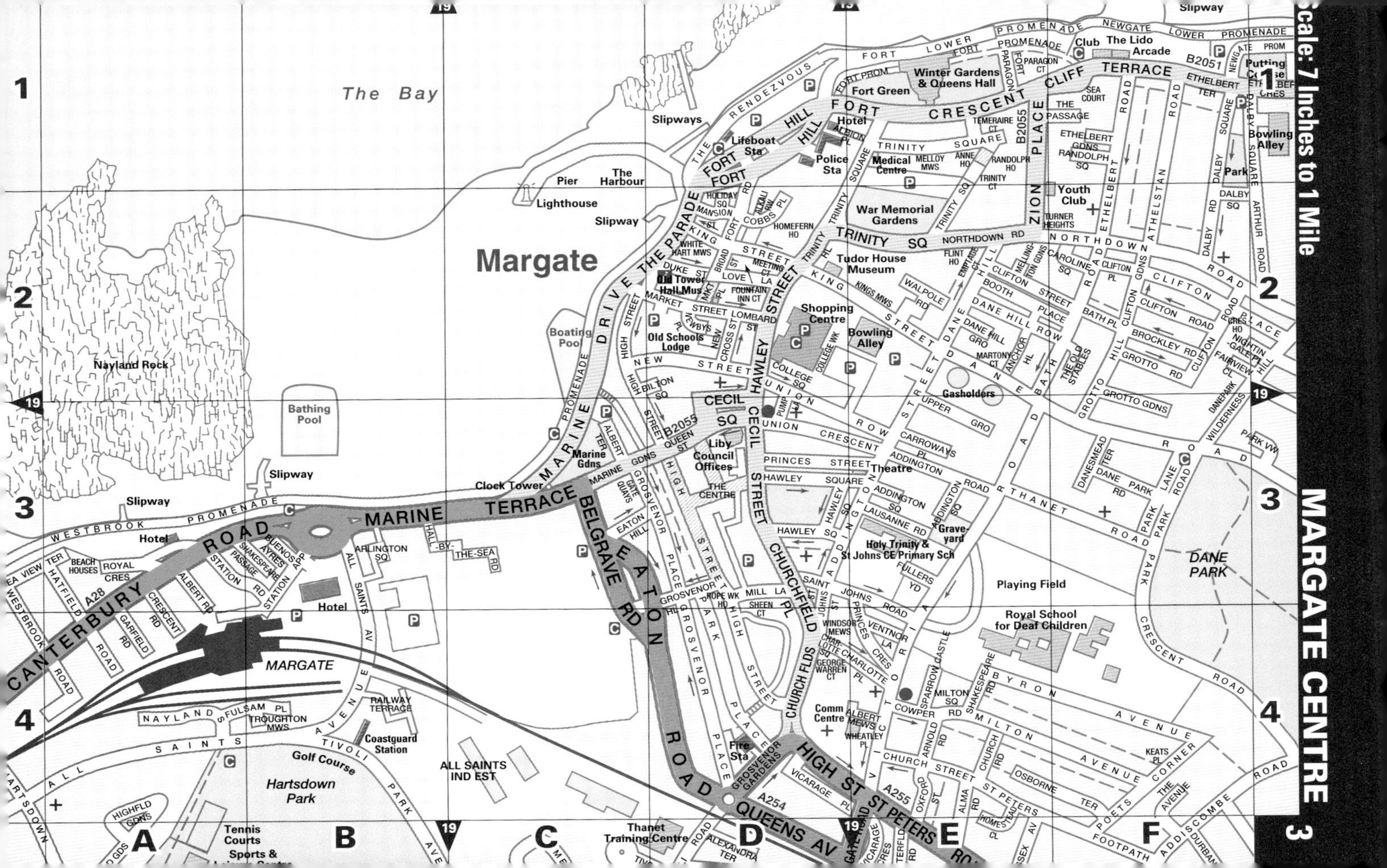
Margate
The Bay
The Harbour
Pier
Lighthouse
Slipway
Slipways
Nayland Rock
Bathing Pool
Boating Pool
Clock Tower
Marine Gdns
MARINE TERRACE
MARINE DRIVE
THE PARADE
CANTERBURY ROAD
A28
BELGRAVE RD
EATON ROAD
QUEENS AV
A254
HIGH ST ST PETERS
A255
CECIL SQ
CECIL STREET
HAWLEY STREET
CHURCHFIELD
CHURCH FLDS
UNION CRESCENT
Shopping Centre
Bowling Alley
Tudor House Museum
War Memorial Gardens
TRINITY SQ
NORTHDOWN RD
ZION PLACE
B2055
B2051
CLIFF TERRACE
FORT CRESCENT
FORT HILL
Fort Green
Winter Gardens & Queens Hall
Police Sta
Lifeboat Sta
Hotel
Liby
Council Offices
THE CENTRE
Theatre
Old Schools Lodge
Old Tower Hall Mus
DANE PARK
DANE ROAD
THANET ROAD
PARK CRESCENT
Playing Field
Royal School for Deaf Children
Gasholders
Holy Trinity & St Johns CE Primary Sch
Grave-yard
Comm Centre
Fire Sta
Thanet Training Centre
ALL SAINTS IND EST
Coastguard Station
Golf Course
Hartsdown Park
Tennis Courts
MARGATE
ALL SAINTS AV
TIVOLI PARK AVE
WESTBROOK PROMENADE
Youth Club
Medical Centre
The Lido
Arcade
Club
Park
Bowling Alley

Scale: 8 Inches to 1 Mile

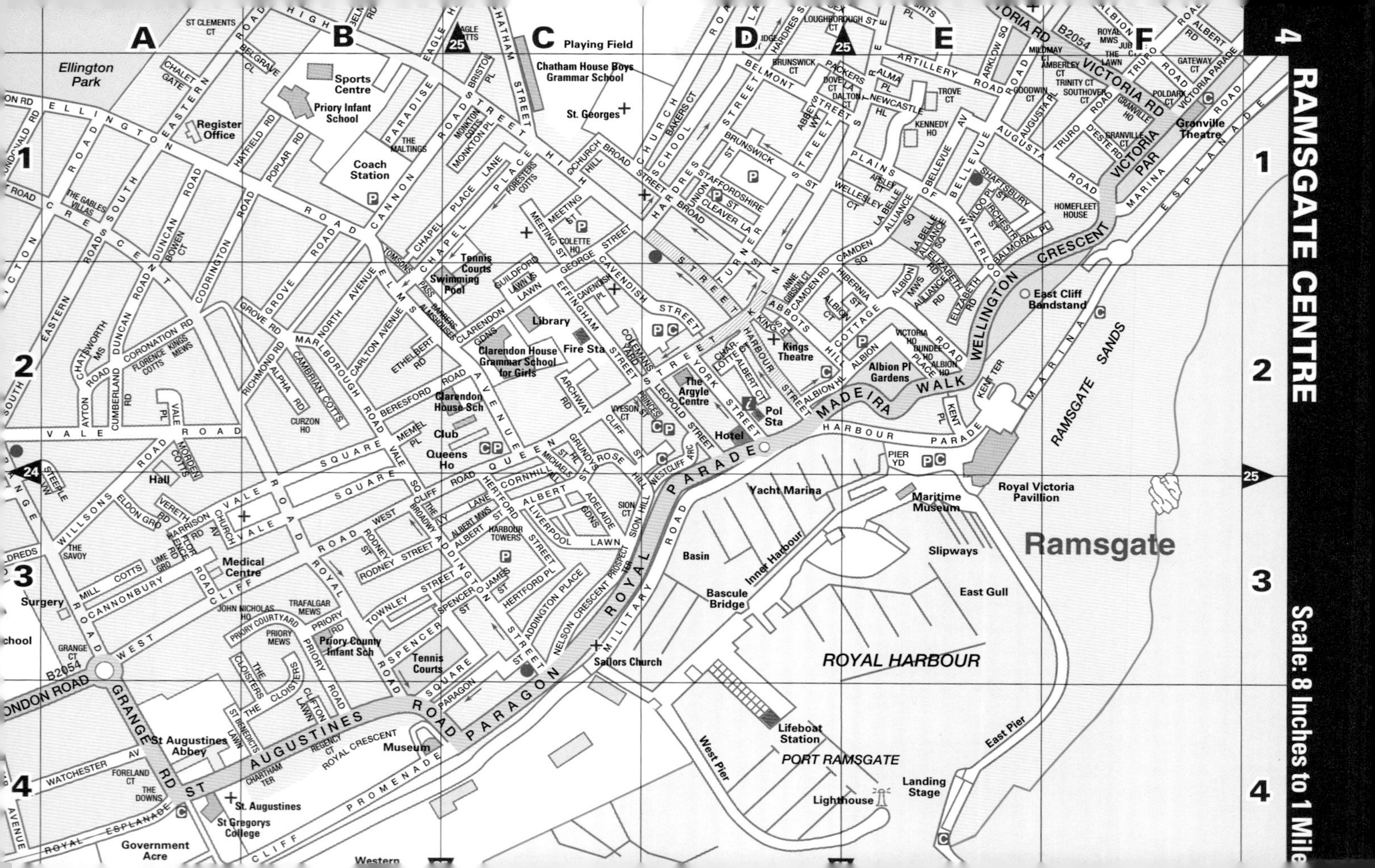

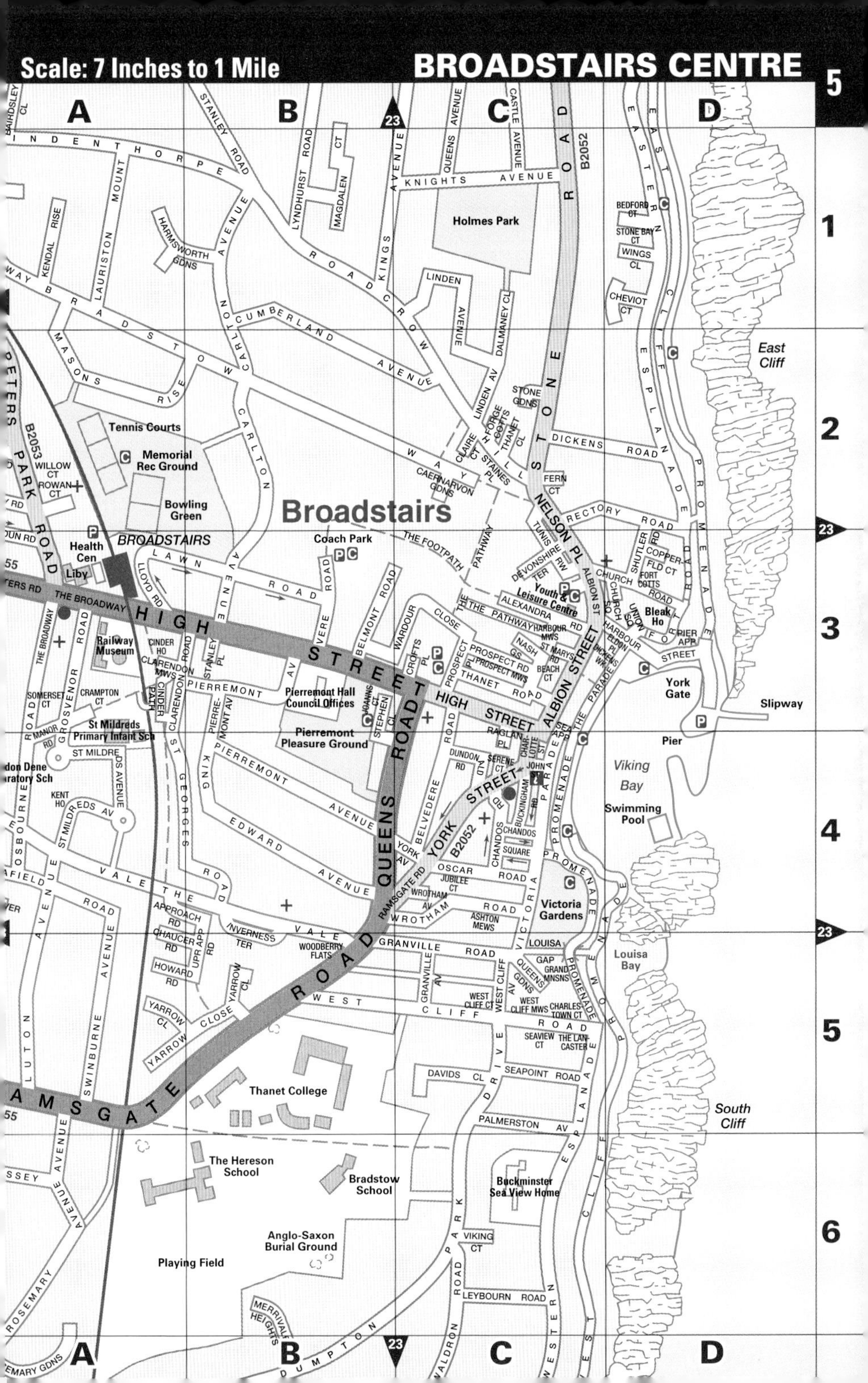
Broadstairs
Holmes Park
Tennis Courts
Memorial Rec Ground
Bowling Green
BROADSTAIRS
Health Cen
Liby
Coach Park
Railway Museum
Pierremont Hall Council Offices
Pierremont Pleasure Ground
St Mildreds Primary Infant Sch
Youth & Leisure Centre
Bleak Ho
York Gate
Slipway
Pier
Viking Bay
Swimming Pool
Victoria Gardens
Louisa Bay
East Cliff
South Cliff
Thanet College
The Hereson School
Bradstow School
Buckminster Sea View Home
Anglo-Saxon Burial Ground
Playing Field
HIGH STREET
QUEENS ROAD
RAMSGATE ROAD
YORK STREET
STONE ROAD
B2052
B2053
23
A
B
C
D
1
2
3
4
5
6

6
CANTERBURY CENTRE
Scale: 8 Inches to 1 Mile
A
B
C
D
1
2
3
4
5
6
CANTERBURY WEST
CANTERBURY EAST
Canterbury
Recreation Centre
Tennis Courts
Playing Field
Leisure Centre
Supermarket
Kingsmead Primary School
Adult Studies Centre
ST JOHNS HOSPITAL
Great Stour
Fallstaff Inn
Westgate
Westgate Hall
Marlowe Theatre
Tower House
Westgate Gardens
Community Support Centre
St Peters Methodist Primary Sch
Beaney Institute Liby & Museum
Greyfriars
Canterbury Museum
The Canterbury Tales
K.C.C. Offices
MARLOWE ARCADE
WHITEFRIARS SHOPPING CENTRE
St Georges Tower
Christ Church Gate
CHRISTCHURCH CATHEDRAL
The Old Palace
The Deanery
Kings School
Norman Staircase
The Forens
Payne Smith Primary Sch
Quenin Gate
International Study Centre
Roman Museum
Magistrate Cort
Hotel
Cinema
Bus Station
Fire Station
Police Station
Health Centre
Multi Storey
Norman Castle
Dane John Gardens
Dane John Mound
City Wall
St Peters Roundabout
ST DUNSTANS ST
ST PETERS PLACE
RHEIMS WAY
PIN HILL
RHODAUS TOWN
UPPER BRIDGE ST
LWR BRIDGE ST
BROAD STREET
MILITARY RD
ST GEORGES PLACE
WINCHEAP
A290
A2050
A28
A257
ST RADIGUNDS STREET
THE BOROUGH
NORTHGATE
HIGH STREET
ST PETERS STREET
ST MARGARETS STREET
ST GEORGES STREET
CASTLE STREET
WATLING STREET
STATION ROAD WEST
STATION ROAD EAST
ST STEPHENS ROAD
NORTH LANE
POUND LANE
ROPER ROAD
WHITEHALL ROAD
OLD DOVER ROAD
NUNNERY FIELDS
OATEN HILL
LANSDOWN ROAD
NORMAN ROAD
CLAREMONT PLACE
MARTYRS FIELD ROAD
GORDON ROAD
NEW STREET
TUDOR ROAD
YORK ROAD
SIMMONDS ROAD
31
35

Caravan Parks
APPLEGARTH PK (Residential Chalet Park)
SALTER LANE
Caravan Parks
ROWAN TREE PK
DEWINDS
THISTLE DR
TRADEWINDS
WRAIK HILL
THE CHAUCER BSNS PK
P.H.
Motel
A299
A290
THANET
MONTPELIER AV
Riding School
WAY
THANET
The Oaks
THE CHALET
Seasalter Dairy Farm
WILLOW ROAD
HILL
ROYAL AV
WILLOW RD
LADYSMITH RD
Willow Wood
SUNNYSIDE RD
WELLINGTON ST
MARLBOROUGH RD
CLAPHAM
A290
Clapham Hill
GOLDEN HILL
LANE
HARRIETS CORNER
PILGRIMS LANE
SEASALTER
Elmcroft
HILL
Pye Alley Farm
BOGSHOLE LANE
WRAIK HILL
Fox's Cross
PYE ALLEY LANE
PEAN
A299
FOXS CROSS ROAD
Yorkletts
FOXS CROSS ROAD
Holme Lodge Farm
Court Lees Farm
Court Lees Manor
Oakhurst Court Farm
PEAN CT RD
BARN CL
GLEN WALK
CHILDGATE RD
FORD WALK
WALK
DARGATE
COOMBE
Coombe Wood
CARLTON RD
HILL
Marley Wood
Pean Hill
Ellenden Wood
A290
1
2
3
4
A
B
C
D
E
F

A
B
C
D
1
2
3
4
5
6
Whitstable Bay
The Oaze
Seasalter
COASTGUARD ALLEY
WAVE CREST
DANIELS CT
WEST BEACH
ISLAND
SAXON SHORE
Golf
SEASALTER BEACH
JOY LANE
GENESTA
METEOR
VALKYRIE
CUNDISHALL CL
Joy Lane Schools
COLUMBIA
SHAMROCK AV
SUNRAY AVENUE
CYPRESS CL
BRITANNIA
SCEPTRE WY
APRIL RISE
NORVIEW RD
SHEARWATER
OSPREY CL
HAWK CL
GRIMTHORPE
MARTINDOWN
ASHURST AV
ADMIRALTY WK
FAIRWAY CRES
PARADE
MEDINA AV
FLORENCE AVENUE
GEORGES AV
ALPHEGE CL
SOMERSET CL
CORYLUS DR
DORSET CL
FIELD VIEW
SANDPIPER ROAD
SWALLOW AV
GOLDCREST WK
LINNET AV
SUNSET CL
SHERWOOD
SHEPPEY VW
LEYSDOWN VW
POLLARD
SANDEND PL
HARTY FERRY VW
THE OAZE
PRESTON
ALLAN RD
HODGSON RD
BOWYER RD
ST MARYS GROVE
Caravan Park
Blue Anchor (P.H.)
Club
FAVERSHAM ROAD
Caravan Park
Comm' Centre
LUCERNE DR
BEACONSFIELDS
LUCERNE DRIVE
ASHLEY DR
JOY ROAD
HAZLEMERE
EDEN ROAD
MACDONALD
FOX DENE RD
WAUCHOPE RD
MILNER
GATE ACRE RD
KIMBERLEY GROVE
ROBERTS RD
LADYSMITH GRO
FAVERSHAM
THE GRANGE
CHANCTONBURY CHASE
ST MARGARETS CL
PARADE
CORDINGHAM CL
NIGHTINGALE AVENUE
CAROLINE CL
ANTHONY CRES
IBIS CL
SPEEDWELL RD
TRILBY WY
EMELINA WY
FREEMANS
HERITAGE CL
FAVOURITE WK
JAYNE WK
NATIVE
ROYAL
PORTLIGHT PL
TRADEWINDS
THE OAKS
SPEEDWELL
MAJOR CL
ROWAN TREE PK
THISTLE DR
CHURCH LANE
ROAD
SEASALTER LANE
APPLEGARTH PK (Residential Chalet Park)
Caravan Parks
Caravan Parks
Seasalter Level
THANET WAY
WRAIK HILL
A299
7

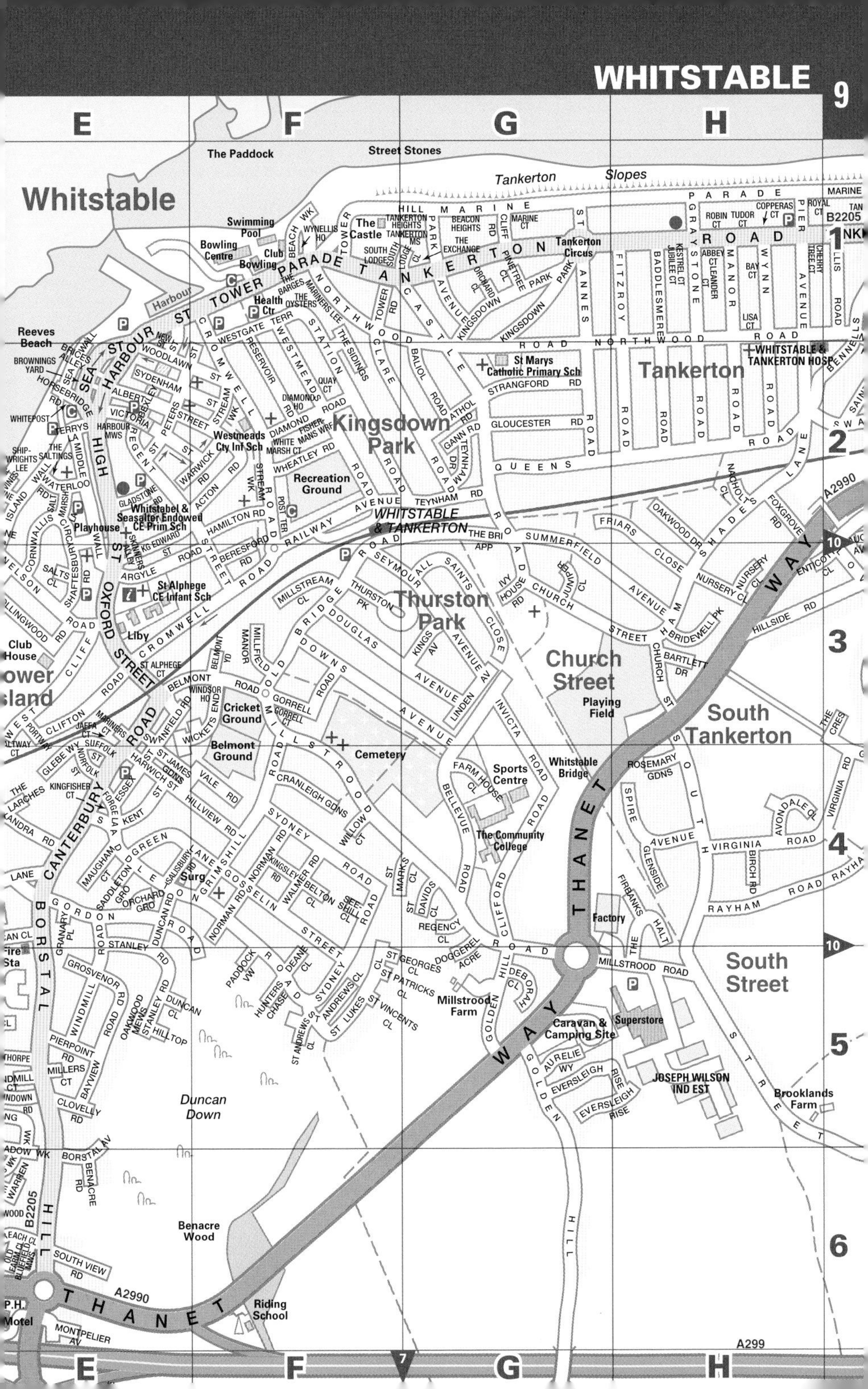
E
F
G
H
The Paddock
Street Stones
Tankerton Slopes
Whitstable
Swimming Pool
Bowling Centre
Club
Bowling
The Castle
Harbour
Reeves Beach
Health Ctr
Tankerton Circus
Tankerton
WHITSTABLE & TANKERTON HOSP
St Marys Catholic Primary Sch
Kingsdown Park
Westmeads Cty Inf Sch
Recreation Ground
WHITSTABLE & TANKERTON
Whitstabel & Seasalter Endowed CE Prim Sch
Playhouse
St Alphege CE Infant Sch
Liby
Thurston Park
Church Street
Playing Field
South Tankerton
Cricket Ground
Belmont Ground
Cemetery
Sports Centre
Whitstable Bridge
The Community College
Surg
Factory
South Street
Millstrood Farm
Caravan & Camping Site
Superstore
JOSEPH WILSON IND EST
Brooklands Farm
Duncan Down
Benacre Wood
Riding School
Motel
TOWER PARADE
TANKERTON ROAD
MARINE PARADE
NORTHWOOD ROAD
HIGH ST
OXFORD STREET
CANTERBURY ROAD
BORSTAL HILL
THANET WAY
A2990
A299
B2205
QUEENS ROAD
MILLSTROOD ROAD
SOUTH STREET
GOLDEN HILL
1
2
3
4
5
6
10
7

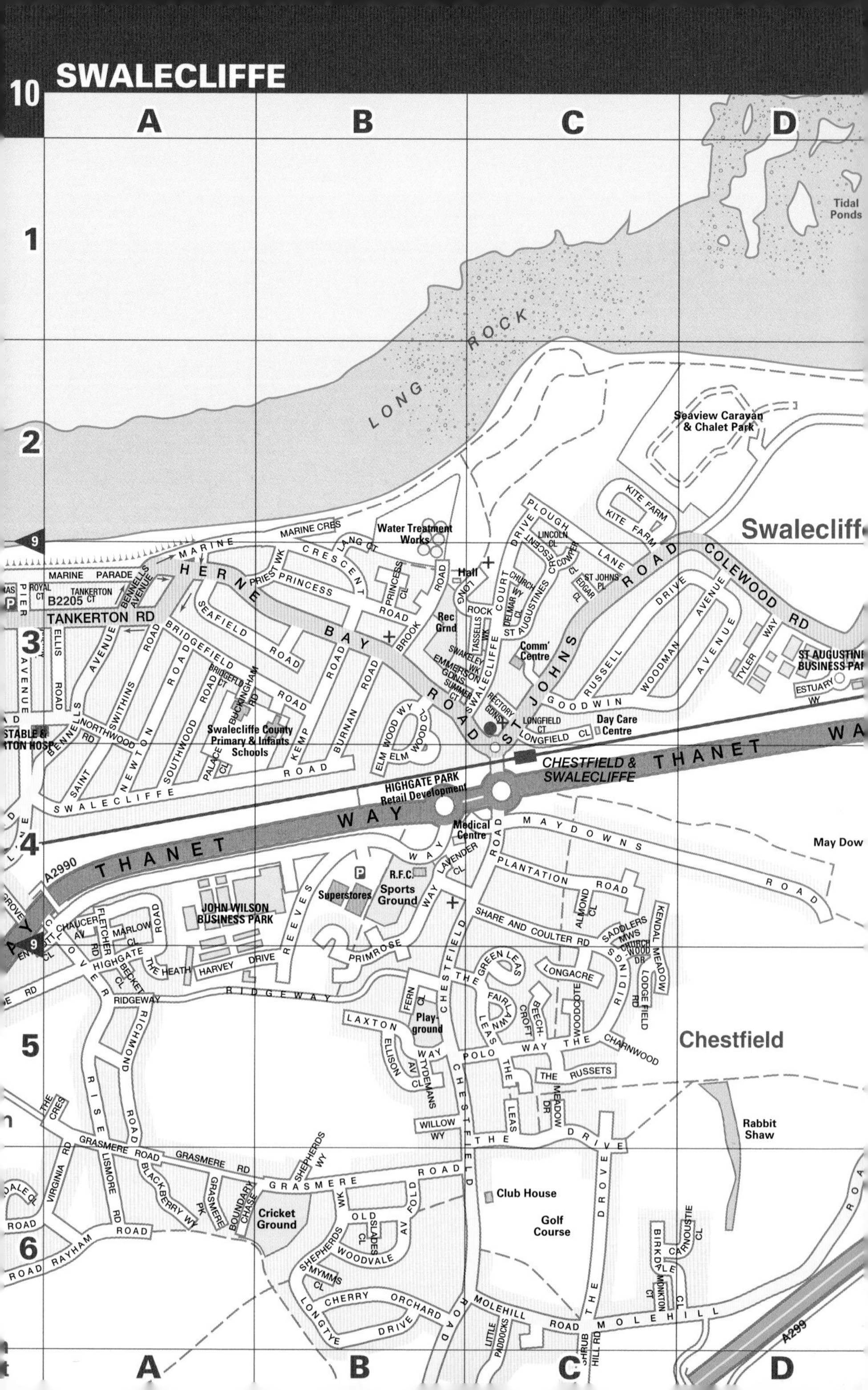
A
B
C
D
1
2
3
4
5
6
Tidal Ponds
LONG ROCK
Seaview Caravan & Chalet Park
Swalecliffe
Water Treatment Works
MARINE CRES
MARINE PARADE
HERNE BAY ROAD
B2205
TANKERTON RD
PRINCESS CRESCENT
SEAFIELD ROAD
BRIDGEFIELD ROAD
Hall
Rec Grnd
Comm' Centre
Day Care Centre
ST JOHNS ROAD
COLEWOOD RD
PLOUGH LANE
KITE FARM
ST AUGUSTINES BUSINESS PARK
Swalecliffe County Primary & Infants Schools
CHESTFIELD & SWALECLIFFE
THANET WAY
HIGHGATE PARK Retail Development
Medical Centre
A2990
MAYDOWNS ROAD
May Dow
JOHN WILSON BUSINESS PARK
Superstores
R.F.C. Sports Ground
PLANTATION ROAD
SHARE AND COULTER RD
Play-ground
Chestfield
Rabbit Shaw
CHESTFIELD ROAD
RIDGEWAY
GRASMERE ROAD
Cricket Ground
Club House
Golf Course
THE DRIVE
THE DROVE
MOLEHILL ROAD
RAYHAM ROAD
A299
CHERRY ORCHARD DRIVE

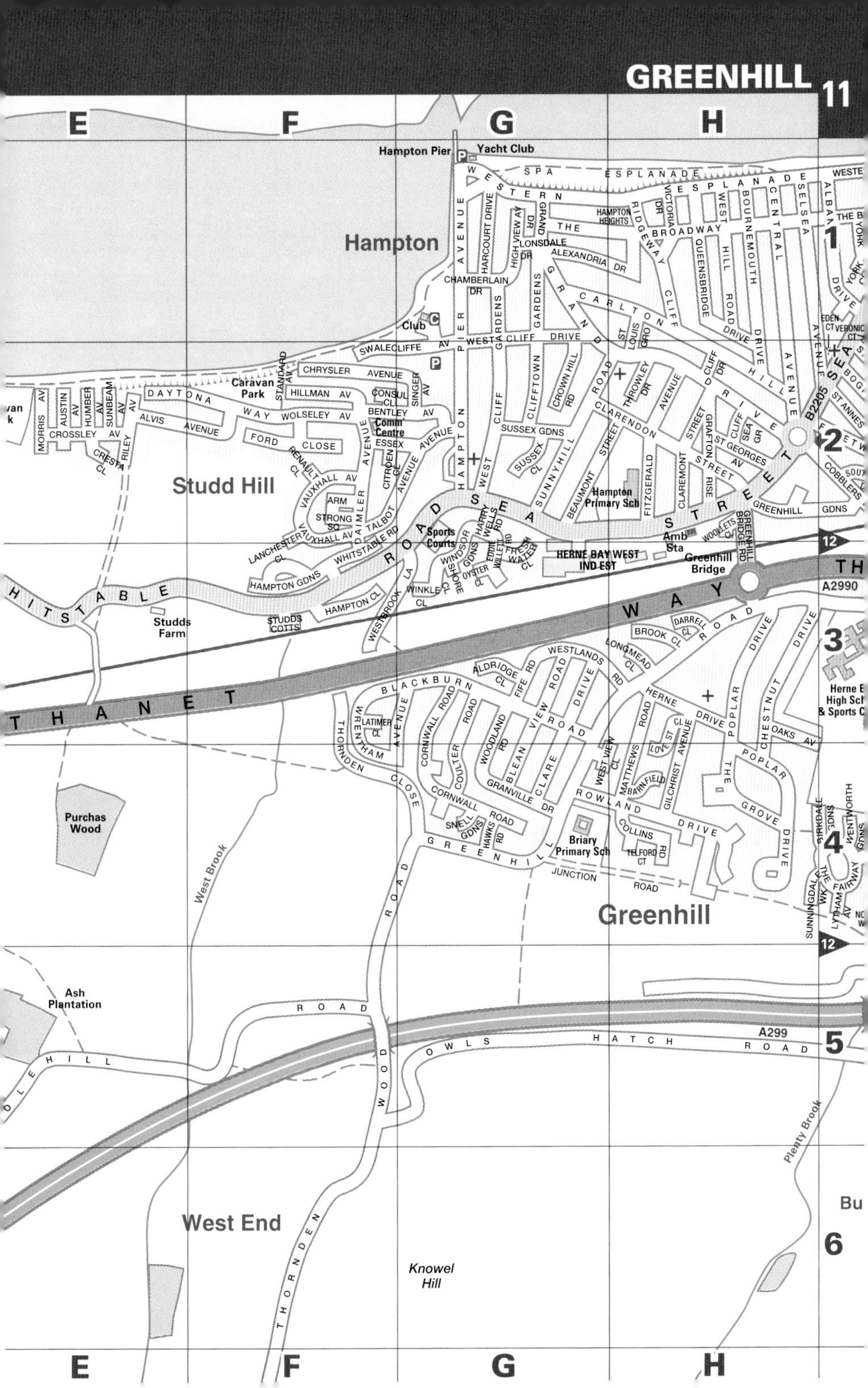
Hampton Pier
Yacht Club
Hampton
Club
Caravan Park
Comm Centre
Studd Hill
Sports Courts
Hampton Primary Sch
Amb Sta
HERNE BAY WEST IND EST
Greenhill Bridge
Studds Farm
STUDDS COTTS
Herne Bay High Sch & Sports C
Purchas Wood
West Brook
Briary Primary Sch
Greenhill
Ash Plantation
West End
Knowel Hill
Plenty Brook
SPA ESPLANADE
WESTERN ESPLANADE
HAMPTON PIER AVENUE
HARCOURT DRIVE
HIGH VIEW AV
GRAND DR
LONSDALE DR
ALEXANDRIA DR
THE BROADWAY
HAMPTON HEIGHTS
RIDGEWAY
VICTORIA DR
WEST CLIFF
QUEENSBRIDGE DRIVE
HILL ROAD
BOURNEMOUTH DRIVE
CENTRAL AVENUE
SELSEA AVENUE
CHAMBERLAIN DR
GARDENS
GRAND DRIVE
CARLTON HILL
ST LOUIS GRO
SWALECLIFFE AV
WEST CLIFF DRIVE
CHRYSLER AVENUE
HILLMAN AV
CONSUL CL
SINGER AV
STANDARD AV
BENTLEY AV
ESSEX AVENUE
DAYTONA WAY
WOLSELEY AV
ALVIS AVENUE
FORD CLOSE
RENAULT CL
MORRIS AV
AUSTIN AV
HUMBER AV
SUNBEAM AV
CROSSLEY AV
CRESTA CL
RILEY
VAUXHALL AV
ARM STRONG SQ
DAIMLER AVENUE
CITROEN CL
TALBOT
LANCHESTER CL
WHITSTABLE RD
HAMPTON GDNS
HAMPTON CL
WESTBROOK LA
WINKLE CL
WINDSOR GDNS
SHORE CL
OYSTER CL
HARRY WELLS RD
EDDIE WILLETT RD
FRESH WATER CL
CLIFFTOWN GARDENS
CROWN HILL RD
CLIFF
SUSSEX GDNS
SUSSEX CL
SUNNYHILL ROAD
BEAUMONT STREET
CLARENDON
THROWLEY DR
AVENUE
FITZGERALD
CLAREMONT STREET
GRAFTON RISE
CLIFF SEA GR
ST GEORGES AV
STREET
RIVE
CLIFF DR
B2205
SEA STREET
GREENHILL GDNS
WOOLLETS CL
GREENHILL BRIDGE RD
WHITSTABLE ROAD
THANET WAY
A2990
DARRELL CL
BROOK CL
ROAD
LONGMEAD CL
WESTLANDS RD
ALDRIDGE CL
FIFE RD
BLACKBURN
VIEW ROAD
DRIVE
LATIMER CL
WRENTHAM AVENUE
THORNDEN CLOSE
CORNWALL ROAD
COULTER ROAD
WOODLAND RD
BLEAN
CLARE
GRANVILLE DR
SNELL GDNS
HAWKS RD
GREENHILL
HERNE DRIVE
WEST VIEW CL
MATTHEWS ROAD
LOVE ST CL
BARNFIELD
GILCHRIST AVENUE
ROWLAND DRIVE
COLLINS RD
TELFORD CT
POPLAR DRIVE
CHESTNUT DRIVE
OAKS AV
THE GROVE
JUNCTION ROAD
SUNNINGDALE
BIRKDALE
WENTWORTH GDNS
FAIRWAY
LYTHAM AV
THE WK
THORNDEN WOOD ROAD
A299
OWLS HATCH ROAD
HILL
EDEN CT
VERONICA CT
ST ANNES
COBBLERS
YORK
ALBANY
THE B
WESTE
E
F
G
H
1
2
3
4
5
6
12

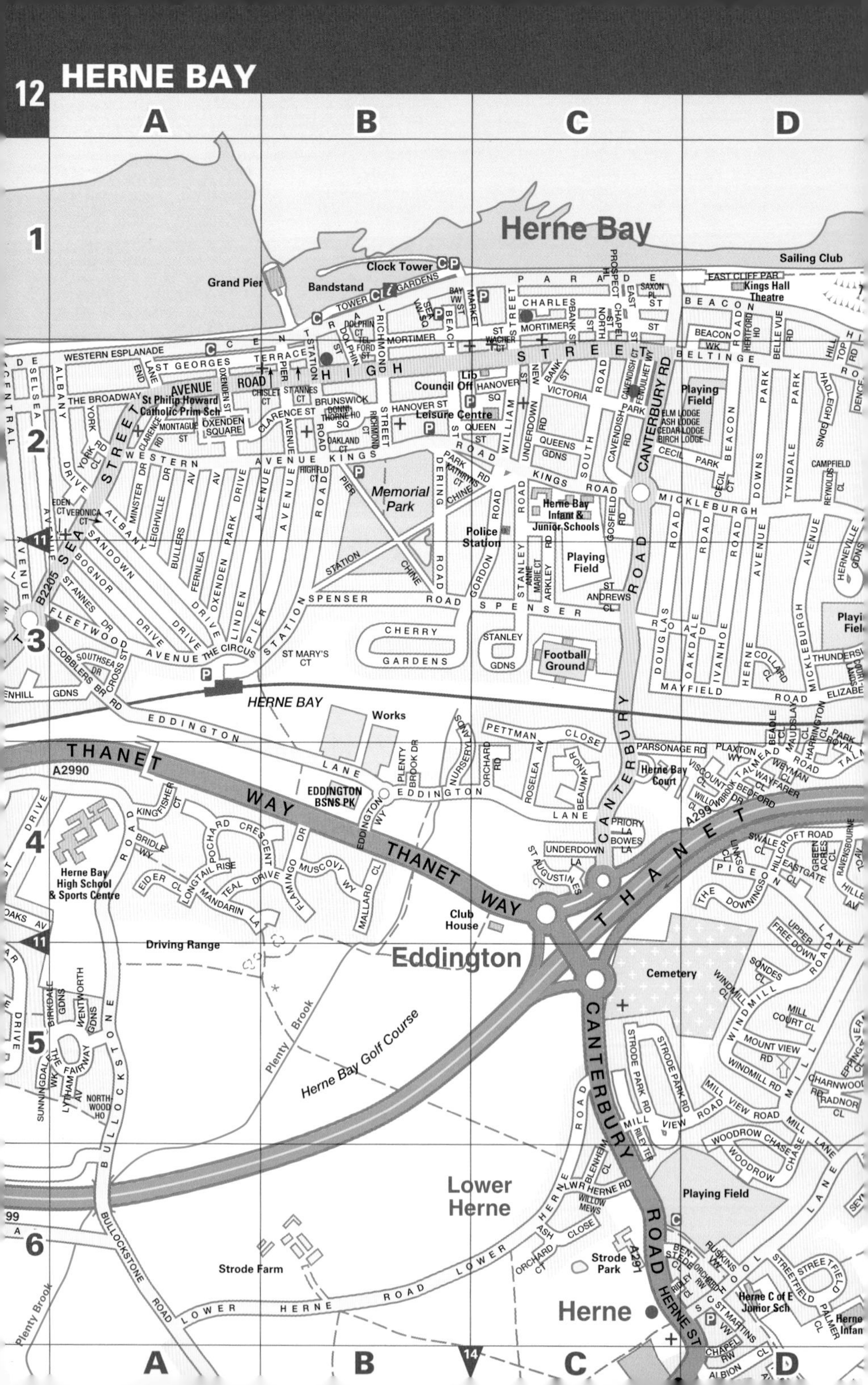
12
HERNE BAY
A
B
C
D
1
2
3
4
5
6
Herne Bay
Sailing Club
Clock Tower
Grand Pier
Bandstand
Kings Hall Theatre
EAST CLIFF PAR
WESTERN ESPLANADE
CENTRAL PARADE
HIGH STREET
BELTINGE
MORTIMER ST
CHARLES ST
BEACON RD
ST GEORGES TERRACE
AVENUE ROAD
THE BROADWAY
St Philip Howard Catholic Prim Sch
OXENDEN SQUARE
MONTAGUE ST
BRUNSWICK SQ
CLARENCE ST
HANOVER ST
Council Off
Lib
Leisure Centre
QUEEN ST
WILLIAM ST
VICTORIA PARK
QUEENS GDNS
Playing Field
ELM LODGE
ASH LODGE
CEDAR LODGE
BIRCH LODGE
CECIL PARK
CANTERBURY RD
WESTERN AVENUE
KINGS ROAD
Memorial Park
MICKLEBURGH HILL
Herne Bay Infant & Junior Schools
Police Station
SEA STREET
ALBANY DRIVE
SANDOWN DRIVE
BOGNOR DRIVE
MINSTER DR
LEIGHVILLE DR
BULLERS AV
FERNLEA AV
OXENDEN PARK DRIVE
LINDEN AVENUE
PIER AVENUE
STATION CHINE
SPENSER ROAD
CHERRY GARDENS
STANLEY GDNS
Football Ground
ST MARY'S CT
THE CIRCUS
FLEETWOOD AVENUE
COBBLERS BR RD
B2205
HERNE BAY
Works
EDDINGTON LANE
EDDINGTON BSNS PK
PETTMAN CLOSE
PARSONAGE RD
Herne Bay Court
DOUGLAS RD
OAKDALE RD
IVANHOE RD
MAYFIELD
THANET WAY
A2990
A299
KINGFISHER CT
POCHARD CRESCENT
BRIDLE WY
LONGTAIL RISE
TEAL DRIVE
EIDER CL
MANDARIN LA
FLAMINGO DR
MUSCOVY WY
MALLARD CL
Herne Bay High School & Sports Centre
Club House
Driving Range
Eddington
Cemetery
Plenty Brook
Herne Bay Golf Course
BULLOCKSTONE ROAD
CANTERBURY ROAD
STRODE PARK RD
MILL VIEW ROAD
WINDMILL RD
Playing Field
Lower Herne
LOWER HERNE ROAD
Strode Farm
Strode Park
Herne
HERNE ST
Herne C of E Junior Sch
A291
14
11

E
F
G
H
1
2
3
4
5
6
Saxon Shore Way
Wantsum Walk
Beltinge Cliff
Beltinge
Bishopstone
Broomfield
Hunters Forstal
Surgery
Maystreet Bridge
Bogshole Bridge
Blacksole Bridge
Blacksole Farm
Maystreet Cross
Goldfinch Farm
Heart in Hand Corner
Oxenden House Farm
Oxenden Corner
Hawe Farm
A299
THANET WAY
RECULVER ROAD
RECULVER DRIVE
GLENBERVIE DRIVE
GAINSBOROUGH DR
BISHOPSTONE DR
BISHOPSTONE LANE
MAY STREET
MAYSTREET
SWEECHBRIDGE RD
HEART IN HAND ROAD
MARGATE ROAD
BOGSHOLE LANE
MAY LANE
FORD HILL
HERNE BAY ROAD
CHURCHILL AV
GRANGE ROAD
SEA VIEW ROAD
CLIFF AVENUE
MARITIME AV
CORNWALLIS AV
WILLOW FARM WAY
GORSE LANE
FORSTAL ROAD
CONYNGHAM RD
COVENTRY GARDENS
LANCASTER GARDENS
TERMINUS DRIVE
OSBORNE GARDENS
HOLMSCROFT
ROSEBERY AV
RICHMOND DR
KEAT FARM CL
NEVILLE RD
PETREL CL
PUFFIN RD
Goldfinch CL
HONEYSUCKLE WY
PLOUGH CT
RYE WK
HUNTERS CHASE
SHERWOOD CL
DEAN CROFT
ASHDOWN CL

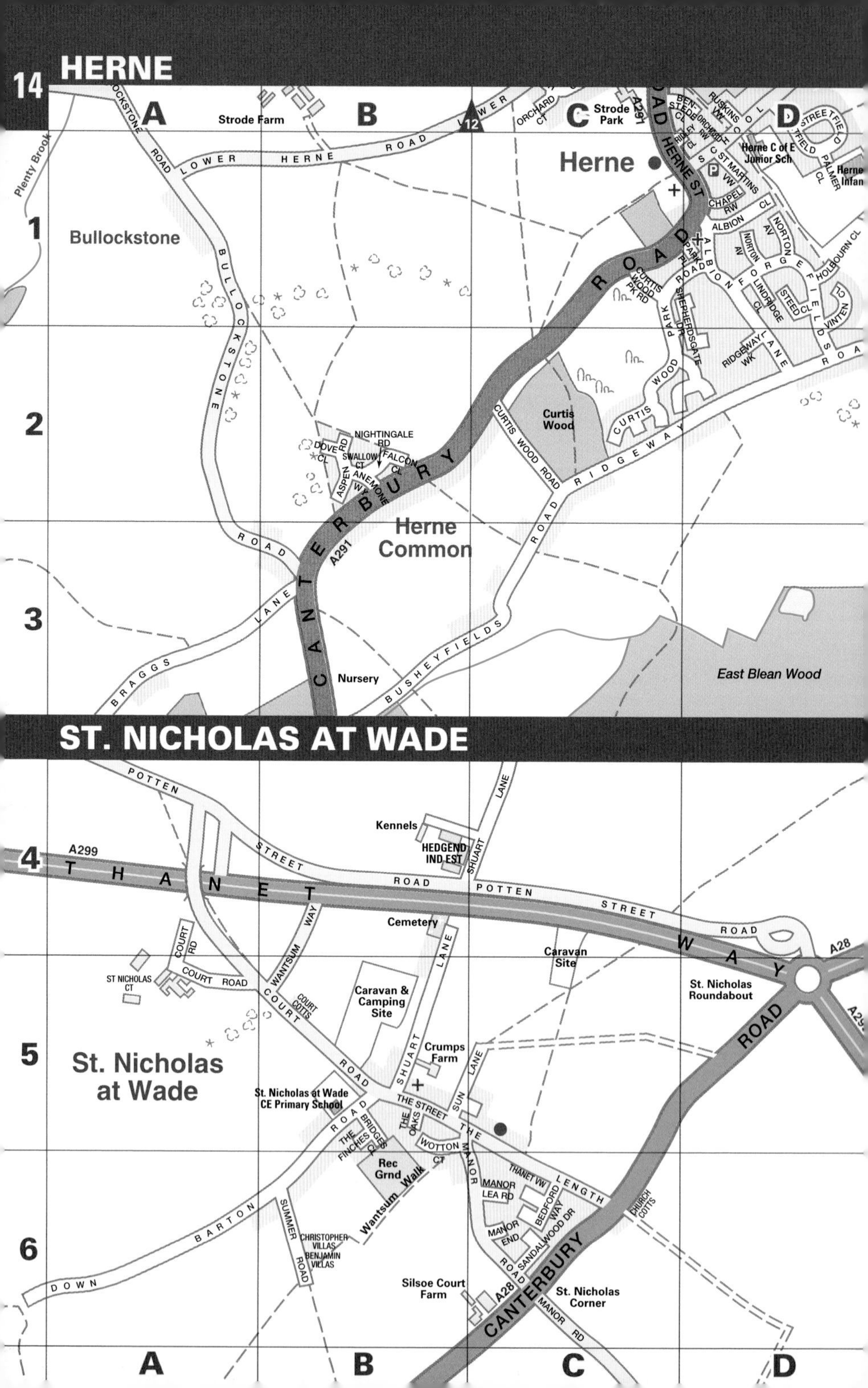
14
HERNE
ST. NICHOLAS AT WADE
A
B
C
D
1
2
3
4
5
6
Strode Farm
Strode Park
Herne
Bullockstone
Plenty Brook
LOWER HERNE ROAD
BULLOCKSTONE ROAD
ORCHARD CT
A291
HERNE ST
RUSKINS VW
BENSTEDE CL
RIDLEY CL
ORCHARD RW
ST MARTINS VW
CHAPEL RW
ALBION CL
ALBION PL
ALBION RD
NORTON AV
NORTON GR
STREETFIELD
PALMER CL
HOLBOURN CL
LINDRIDGE CL
STEED CL
VINTEN CL
FORGEFIELDS
RIDGEWAY WK
LANE
Herne C of E Junior Sch
Herne Infan
PARK RD
PARK DR
SHEPHERDSGATE
CURTIS WOOD PK RD
CURTIS WOOD
CURTIS WOOD ROAD
Curtis Wood
RIDGEWAY
CANTERBURY ROAD
NIGHTINGALE RD
DOVE CL
SWALLOW CT
FALCON CL
ASPEN WY
ANEMONE WY
Herne Common
BRAGGS LANE
ROAD
BUSHEYFIELDS ROAD
Nursery
East Blean Wood
POTTEN STREET
Kennels
HEDGEND IND EST
SHUART LANE
A299
THANET WAY
ROAD
POTTEN STREET ROAD
Cemetery
WANTSUM WAY
COURT RD
COURT ROAD
ST NICHOLAS CT
COURT COTTS
Caravan & Camping Site
Caravan Site
A28
St. Nicholas Roundabout
ROAD
St. Nicholas at Wade
Crumps Farm
SUN LANE
St. Nicholas at Wade CE Primary School
THE STREET
THE OAKS
THE FINCHES
BRIDGES CL
WOTTON CT
Rec Grnd
Wantsum Walk
MANOR ROAD
THANET VW
MANOR LEA RD
BEDFORD WAY
SANDALWOOD DR
MANOR END
THE LENGTH
CHURCH COTTS
BARTON
SUMMER ROAD
CHRISTOPHER VILLAS
BENJAMIN VILLAS
DOWN
Silsoe Court Farm
CANTERBURY
St. Nicholas Corner
MANOR RD

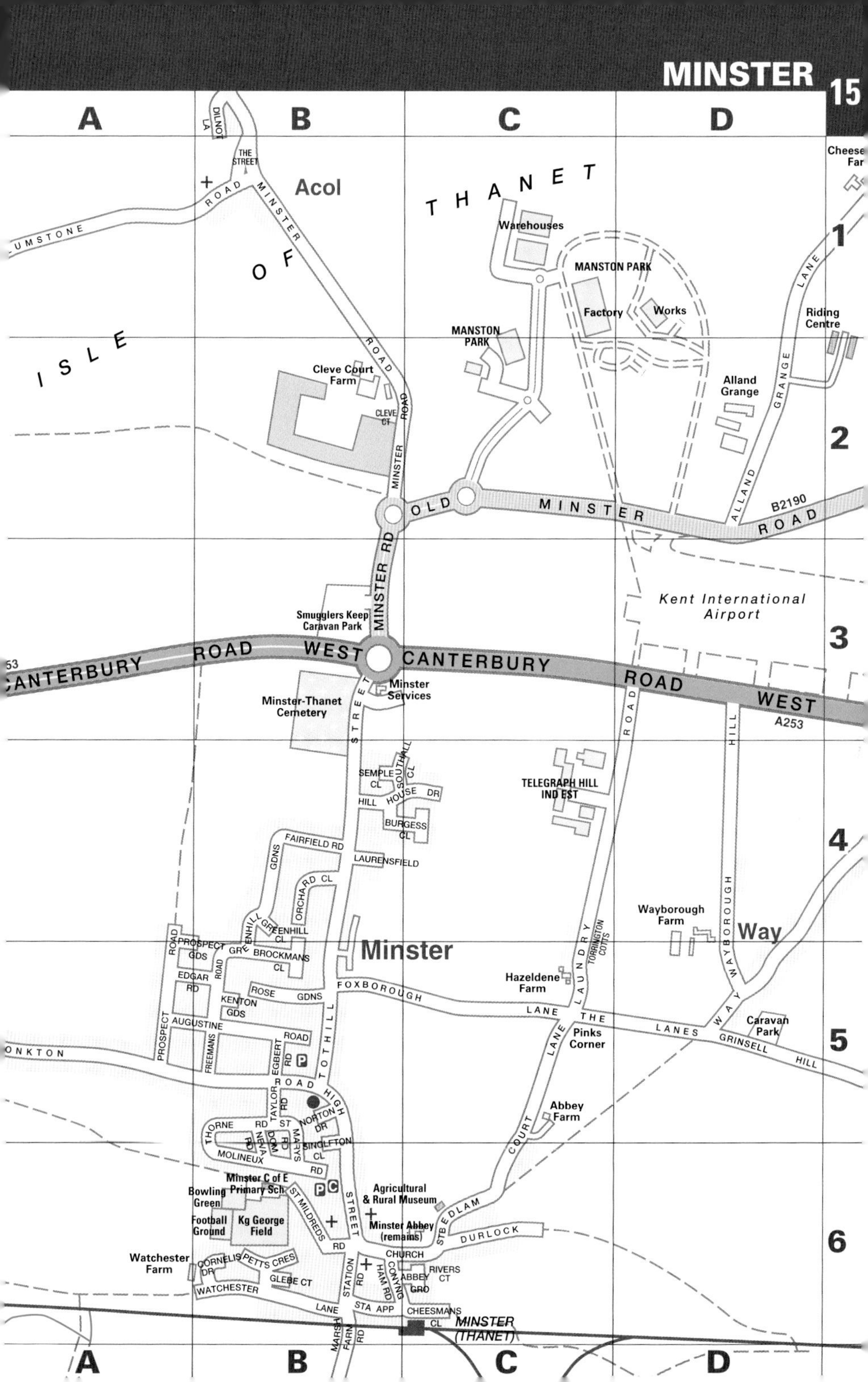
A
B
C
D
1
2
3
4
5
6
Acol
ISLE OF THANET
DILNOT LA
THE STREET
ROAD
MINSTER ROAD
Warehouses
MANSTON PARK
Factory
Works
MANSTON PARK
Cleve Court Farm
CLEVE CT
Riding Centre
Alland Grange
GRANGE
LANE
ALLAND
OLD MINSTER ROAD
B2190
MINSTER RD
Kent International Airport
Smugglers Keep Caravan Park
CANTERBURY ROAD WEST
A253
Minster Services
Minster-Thanet Cemetery
STREET
SEMPLE CL
SOUTHALL CL
HILL HOUSE DR
BURGESS CL
TELEGRAPH HILL IND EST
FAIRFIELD RD
LAURENSFIELD
ORCHARD CL
GREENHILL CL
GREENHILL GDNS
PROSPECT GDNS
PROSPECT ROAD
BROCKMANS CL
EDGAR RD
ROSE GDNS
KENTON GDS
AUGUSTINE ROAD
FREEMANS
EGBERT RD
TOTHILL
Minster
FOXBOROUGH LANE
Wayborough Farm
Way
WAYBOROUGH HILL
TORRINGTON COTTS
LAUNDRY ROAD
Hazeldene Farm
Pinks Corner
THE LANES
WAY
GRINSELL HILL
Caravan Park
MONKTON
HIGH
TAYLOR RD
NORTON DR
THORNE RD
NEVIA
DOM
ST MARYS RD
SINGLETON CL
MOLINEUX RD
Abbey Farm
COURT LANE
Minster C of E Primary Sch
Bowling Green
Football Ground
Kg George Field
ST MILDREDS RD
Agricultural & Rural Museum
Minster Abbey (remains)
BEDLAM
DURLOCK
CHURCH
Watchester Farm
CORNELIS DR
PETTS CRES
GLEBE CT
WATCHESTER LANE
STATION RD
HAM RD
CONYNG
ABBEY GRO
RIVERS CT
STA APP
CHEESMANS CL
MINSTER (THANET)
MARSH FARM RD
Cheese Far

16
BIRCHINGTON
A
B
C
D
1
2
3
4
5
6
Grenham Bay
Minnis Bay
Paddling Pool
CLIFF
ROAD
PARADE
THE PROMENADE
Wantsum Walk
LARKSCLIFF CT
SEA VIEW HEIGHTS
BAY VIEW HEIGHTS
APRIL RISE
MCKINLAY CT
RINGSLOE CT
SEA POINT
HEREWARD AV
SEA VIEW AV
SEA VIEW ROAD
HAROLD ROAD
THE ALFRED RD
ETHELBERT RD
WALKER LA
FERN DOWN
EGBERT RD
MINNIS ROAD
ARTHUR RD
VIKING CL
CANUTE ROAD
KINGS AVENUE
QUEENS AVENUE
THE HENGIST RD
DARYNGTON AV
DANE RD
HORSA RD
INGOLDSBY ROAD
OLD FARM RD
PRINCES CL
GRENHAM ROAD
GRENHAM BAY AVENUE
RECULVER AVENUE
ST MILDREDS AVENUE
GALLWEY AV
NELSON CT
CUNNINGHAM CRES
DUNCAN DR
CONWAY CL
GRENVILLE GDNS
GREEN ROAD
GRENHAM BAY CT
ANNA PARK
BERKELEY RD
HERSCHELL RD
WILD AIR
DALLINGER RD
BERESFORD AVENUE
GAINSBORO RD
SPENCER
SHAKESPEARE
SEMAPHORE RD
DARWIN RD
LYELL CT
BEACH
ROSSETTI CT
ROSSETTI RD
HUNTING GATE
BIERCE CT
BIRCHINGTON
STA APP
SANDLES RD
MINNIS RD
GORE END CL
MILES WY
THE MALTINGS
UPR
THE MALT HOUSES
CRISPE HO
CLAIRE CT
Gore End Farm
Medical Centre
WALNUT MWS
GORDON SQ
KENT
SURREY GDNS
PROSPECT
RUTLAND GDNS
SUSSEX GDNS
LINCOLN GDNS
GARDENS
DORSET GDNS
DEVON
ESSEX
LANCASTER
MANOR GARDENS
Birchington
MILL LA
MILL ROW
SHAMROCK VILLAS
HAMILTON CT
FLINT COTTS
QUEX
KING
NOTTINGHAM RD
SHERWOOD RD
BROADLEY AV
Reservoirs
Great Brooksend Farm
A28
CANTERBURY ROAD
Brooks End
BROOKSEND COTTS
Little Brooksend Farm
Upper Hale
COLLEGE FARM COTTS
CRISPE ROAD
SEAMARK ROAD
Hale
A
B
C
D

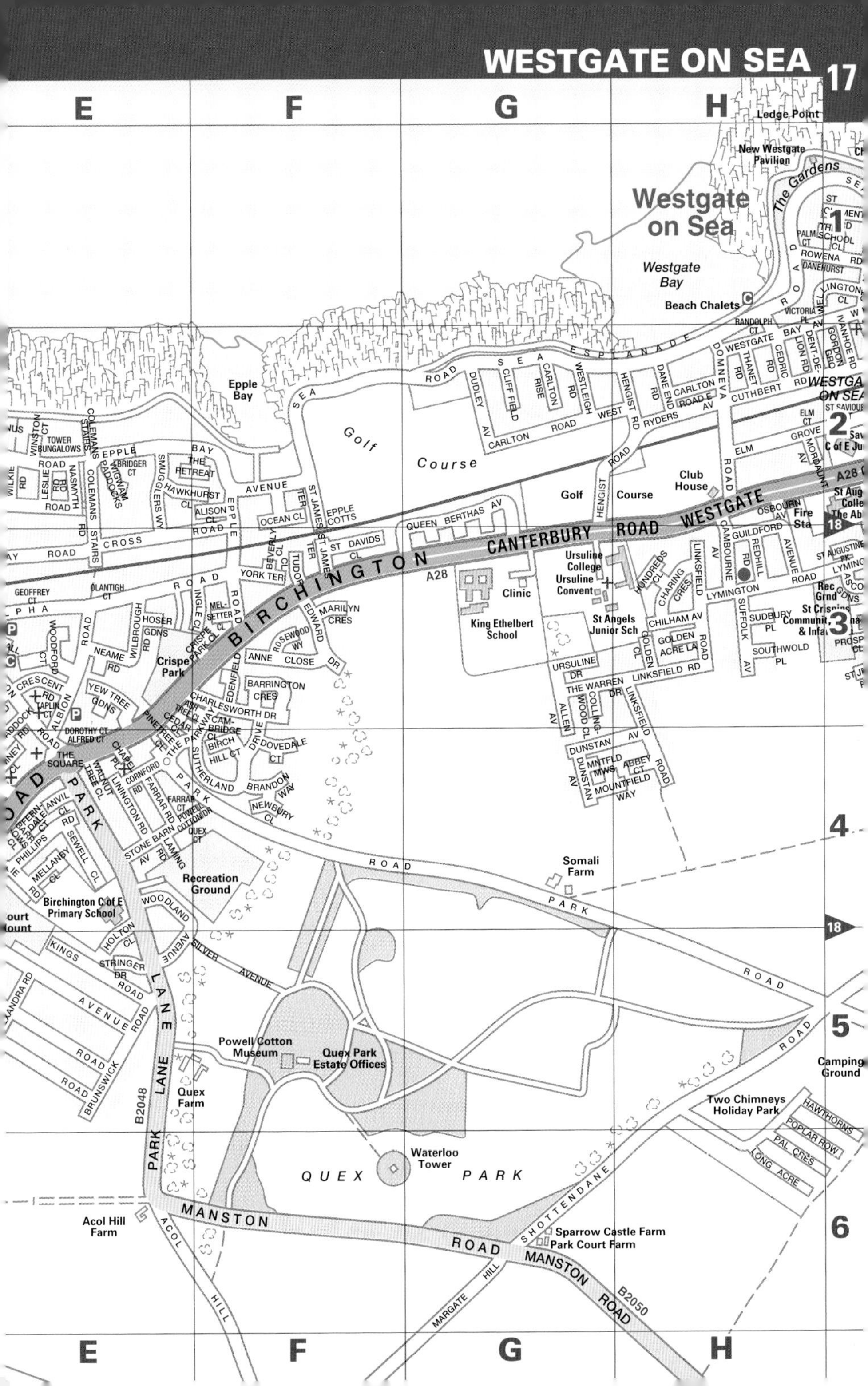
E
F
G
H
Ledge Point
New Westgate Pavilion
Westgate on Sea
Westgate Bay
Beach Chalets
The Gardens
Epple Bay
Golf Course
Club House
CANTERBURY ROAD WESTGATE
BIRCHINGTON
A28
Ursuline College
Ursuline Convent
Clinic
King Ethelbert School
St Angels Junior Sch
Crispe Park
Recreation Ground
Birchington C of E Primary School
Somali Farm
Powell Cotton Museum
Quex Park Estate Offices
Quex Farm
Waterloo Tower
QUEX PARK
Acol Hill Farm
MANSTON ROAD
Sparrow Castle Farm
Park Court Farm
Two Chimneys Holiday Park
Camping Ground
PARK LANE
B2048
B2050
SHOTTENDANE
MARGATE HILL
ACOL HILL
PARK ROAD
1
2
3
4
5
6
18

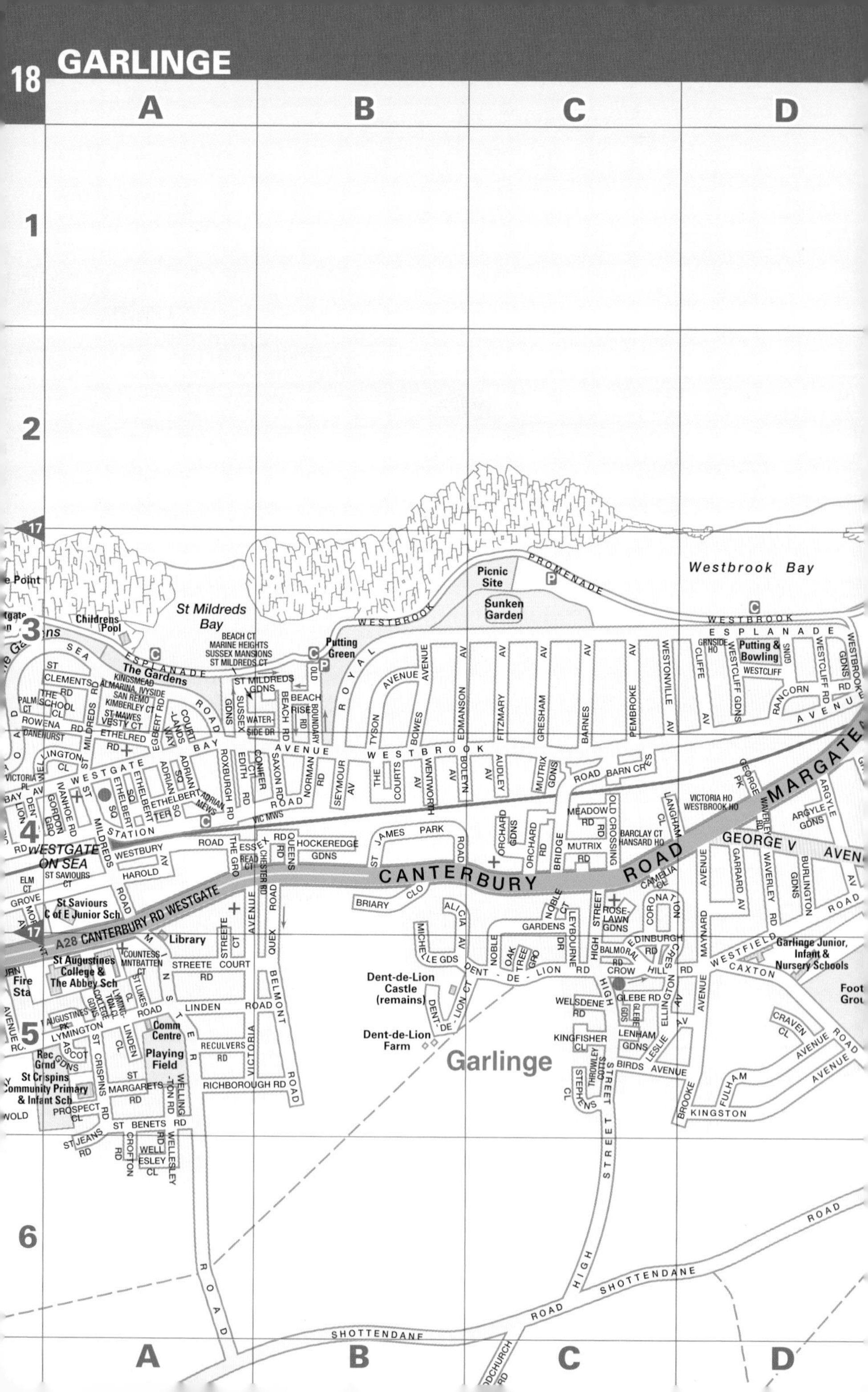
18
GARLINGE
A
B
C
D
1
2
3
4
5
6
17
Westbrook Bay
St Mildreds Bay
Picnic Site
Sunken Garden
PROMENADE
WESTBROOK
ESPLANADE
Putting Green
Putting & Bowling
Childrens Pool
The Gardens
BEACH CT
MARINE HEIGHTS
SUSSEX MANSIONS
ST MILDREDS CT
ROYAL
WESTBROOK AVENUE
CANTERBURY ROAD
MARGATE
GEORGE V AVENUE
A28 CANTERBURY RD WESTGATE
WESTGATE ON SEA
ST MILDREDS
STATION
Library
Fire Sta
St Saviours C of E Junior Sch
St Augustines College & The Abbey Sch
St Crispins Community Primary & Infant Sch
Comm Centre
Playing Field
Rec Grnd
Dent-de-Lion Castle (remains)
Dent-de-Lion Farm
Garlinge
Garlinge Junior, Infant & Nursery Schools
HIGH STREET
SHOTTENDANE ROAD
ST JAMES PARK ROAD
HOCKEREDGE GDNS
VICTORIA AVENUE
QUEX ROAD
BELMONT ROAD
RICHBOROUGH RD
RECULVERS RD
LINDEN ROAD
MINSTER ROAD
DENT-DE-LION RD
BIRDS AVENUE
KINGSTON
FULHAM AVENUE
CRAVEN CL
WESTFIELD
CAXTON
MAYNARD AVENUE
ELLINGTON AV
CORONATION CRES
ROSE-LAWN GDNS
LEYBOURNE DR
BRIDGE RD
OLD CROSSING RD
MEADOW RD
MUTRIX RD
BARN CRES
VICTORIA HO
WESTBROOK HO
BARCLAY CT
HANSARD HO
WESTCLIFF
RANCORN
CLIFFE AV
WESTONVILLE AV
PEMBROKE AV
BARNES AV
GRESHAM AV
FITZMARY AV
EDMANSON AV
BOWES AVENUE
TYSON AVENUE
SEYMOUR AV
NORMAN RD
SAXON RD
CONIFER CT
EDITH RD
ROXBURGH RD
ETHELBERT RD
ADRIAN SQ
ROWENA RD
ETHELRED
PALM CT
ST CLEMENTS RD
BRIARY CLO
ALICIA AV
NOBLE GARDENS
OAK TREE GRO
WELSDENE RD
KINGFISHER CL
LENHAM GDNS
LESLIE AV
GLEBE RD
CROW HILL RD
EDINBURGH RD
BALMORAL RD
STEPHENS CL
BROOKE AV
ST BENETS RD
ST JEANS RD
CROFTON RD
WELLESLEY CL
PROSPECT CL
ASCOT GDNS
LYMINGTON RD
Foot Grou

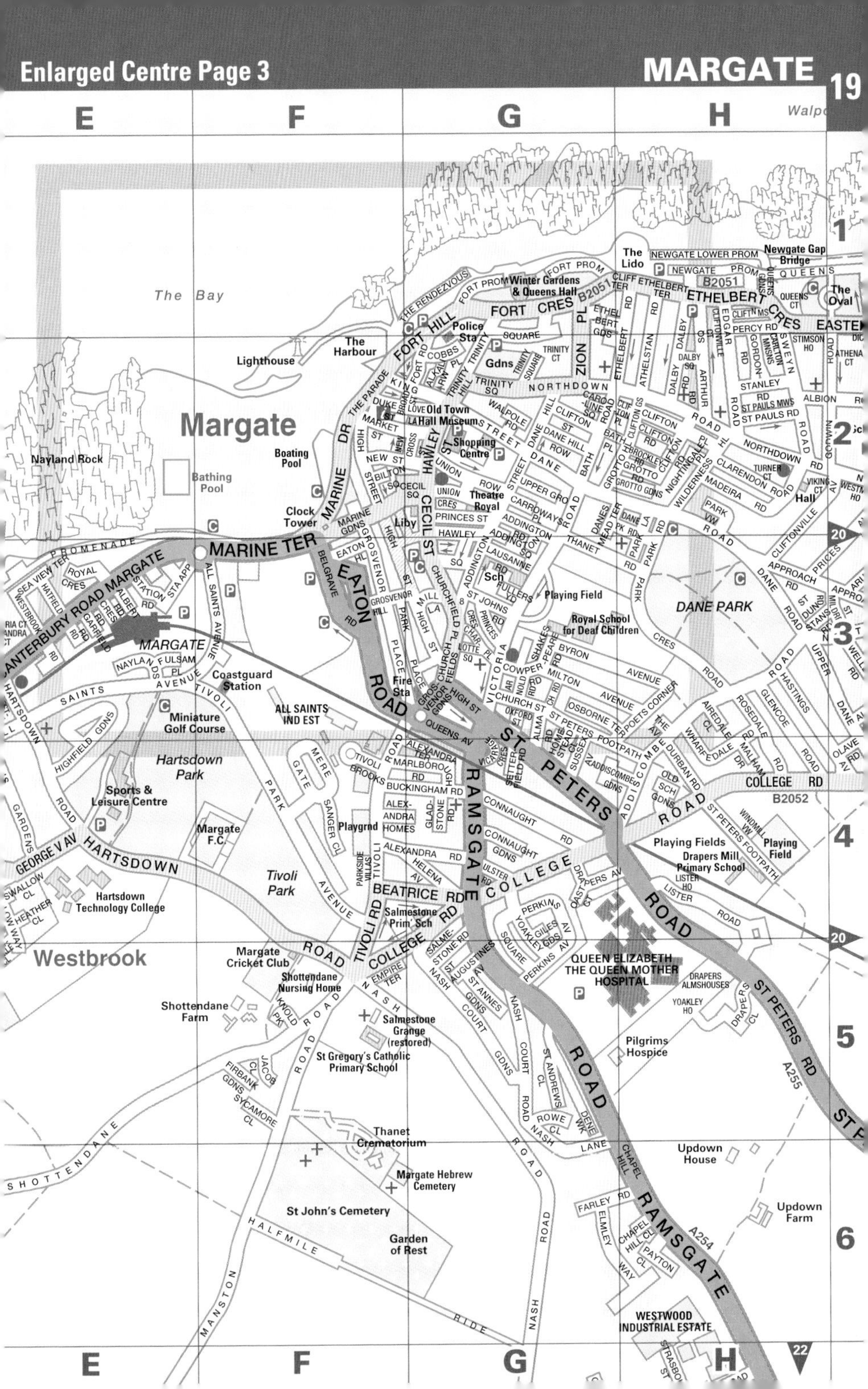
E
F
G
H
The Bay
Lighthouse
The Harbour
Margate
Nayland Rock
Bathing Pool
Boating Pool
Clock Tower
MARINE TER
MARINE DR
FORT HILL
FORT CRES
Winter Gardens & Queens Hall
The Lido
Newgate Gap Bridge
The Oval
ETHELBERT CRES
NORTHDOWN ROAD
Old Town Hall Museum
Shopping Centre
Theatre Royal
Police Sta
Trinity Gdns
CECIL ST
DANE PARK
Playing Field
Royal School for Deaf Children
CANTERBURY ROAD MARGATE
MARGATE
Coastguard Station
ALL SAINTS IND EST
Miniature Golf Course
Hartsdown Park
Sports & Leisure Centre
Margate F.C.
Tivoli Park
HARTSDOWN ROAD
Hartsdown Technology College
Westbrook
Margate Cricket Club
Shottendane Nursing Home
Shottendane Farm
Salmestone Grange (restored)
St Gregory's Catholic Primary School
Thanet Crematorium
Margate Hebrew Cemetery
St John's Cemetery
Garden of Rest
EATON ROAD
ST PETERS ROAD
RAMSGATE ROAD
COLLEGE RD
B2052
Playing Fields
Drapers Mill Primary School
QUEEN ELIZABETH THE QUEEN MOTHER HOSPITAL
DRAPERS ALMSHOUSES
Pilgrims Hospice
Updown House
Updown Farm
WESTWOOD INDUSTRIAL ESTATE
A254
A255
SHOTTENDANE
HALFMILE RIDE
MANSTON
NASH ROAD
1
2
3
4
5
6
20
22

Walpole Bay
Walpole Rocks
Palm Bay
Bathing Pool
Newgate Gap Bridge
Hodges Bridge
The Oval
Bowling Greens
Miniature Golf Course
Palm Bay Primary Sch
Recreation Ground
Cliftonville
Playing Field
Cliftonville Prim' Sch
Laleham Gap School
Northdown
Northdown Park
St Anthonys School
Northdown Primary Sch
Northdown House
East Northdown Farm
Playground
THANET ENTERPRISE CENTRE
Updown Farm
EASTERN ESPLANADE
PALM BAY AVENUE
NORTHDOWN ROAD
MILLMEAD ROAD
COLLEGE RD
ST PETERS RD
NORTHDOWN PK RD
GEORGE HILL RD
QUEEN ELIZABETH AV
PRINCESS MARGARET AV
DANE VALLEY ROAD
ST PETERS FOOTPATH
B2052
B2053
A255

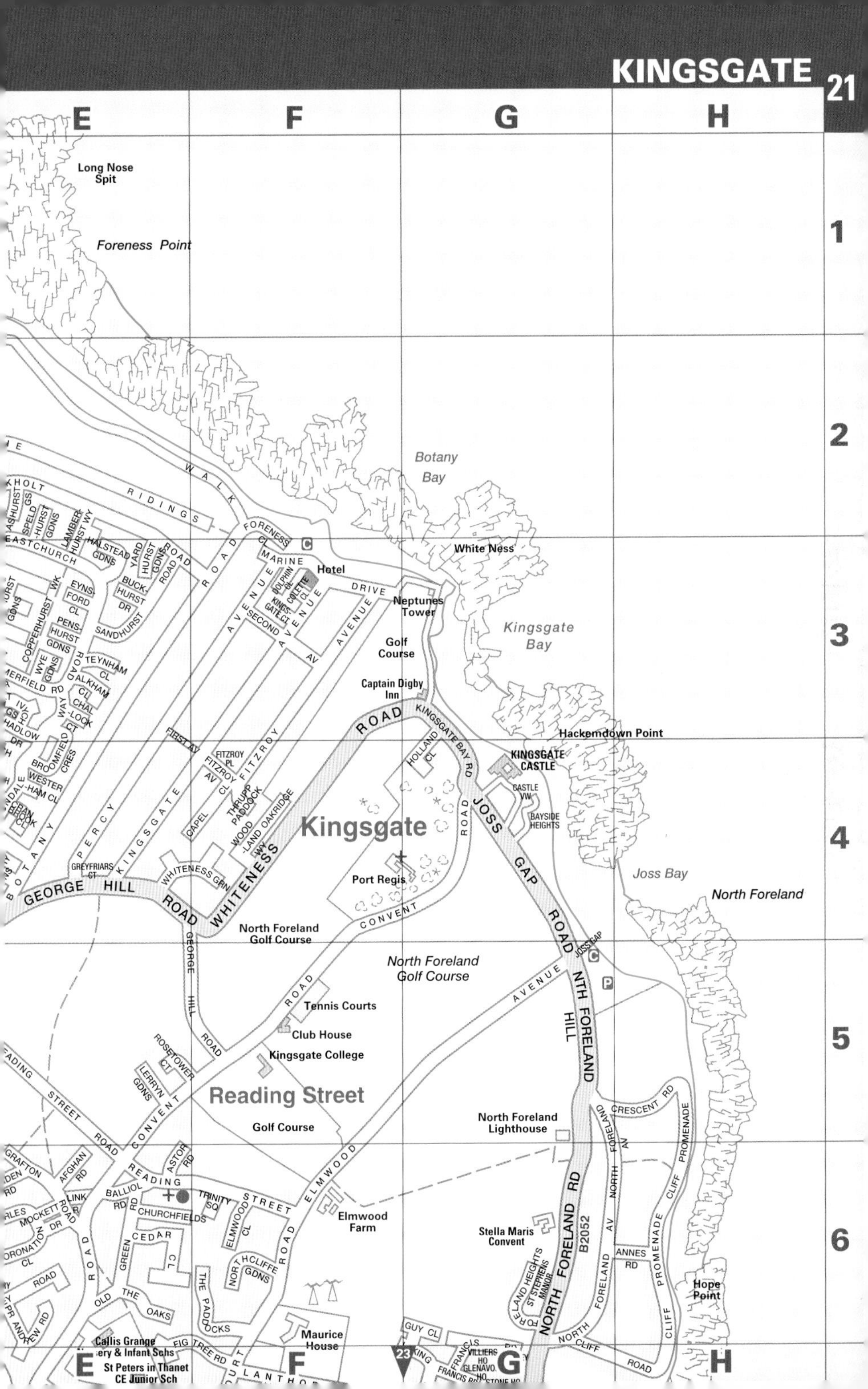
E
F
G
H
1
2
3
4
5
6
Long Nose Spit
Foreness Point
Botany Bay
White Ness
Kingsgate Bay
Hackemdown Point
KINGSGATE CASTLE
Joss Bay
North Foreland
Hotel
Neptunes Tower
Golf Course
Captain Digby Inn
Kingsgate
Port Regis
North Foreland Golf Course
North Foreland Golf Course
Tennis Courts
Club House
Kingsgate College
Reading Street
Golf Course
North Foreland Lighthouse
Elmwood Farm
Stella Maris Convent
Hope Point
Maurice House
Callis Grange
St Peters in Thanet CE Junior Sch
RIDINGS
WALK
FORENESS CL
MARINE DRIVE
SECOND AVENUE
FIRST AV
FITZROY AV
FITZROY PL
KINGSGATE AVENUE
PERCY AVENUE
BOTANY
GEORGE HILL ROAD
WHITENESS ROAD
WHITENESS GRN
GREYFRIARS CT
GEORGE HILL ROAD
CONVENT ROAD
KINGSGATE BAY RD
HOLLAND CL
CASTLE VW
BAYSIDE HEIGHTS
JOSS GAP ROAD
JOSS GAP
NTH FORELAND HILL
NORTH FORELAND RD
B2052
NORTH FORELAND AV
CRESCENT RD
CLIFF PROMENADE
ANNES RD
NORTH CLIFF ROAD
AVENUE
ELMWOOD AVENUE
READING STREET
ROSETOWER CT
LERRYN GDNS
ASTOR RD
BALLIOL RD
TRINITY SQ
CHURCHFIELDS
CEDAR CL
GREEN
ELMWOOD CL
NORTHCLIFFE GDNS
THE PADDOCKS
THE OAKS
FIG TREE RD
GUY CL
KING
23
EASTCHURCH
HALSTEAD GDNS
EYNSFORD CL
PENSHURST GDNS
TEYNHAM CL
ALKHAM CL
CHALLOCK CT
BROOMFIELD CRES
WESTERHAM CL
CRANBROOK CL
BUCKHURST DR
SANDHURST
COPPERHURST WK
CAPEL CL
THRUPP PADDOCK
OAKRIDGE
WOODLAND WY
GRAFTON
AFGHAN RD
LINK
MOCKETT DR
CORONATION CL
OLD

A
B
C
D
1
2
3
4
5
6
20
24
Pilgrims Hospice
Updown House
Updown Farm
ST PETERS RD
A255
FOOTPATH
VALLEY ROAD
BROADLEY
THANET ENTERPRISE CENTRE
B2053
OAKWOOD IND EST
RAMSGATE ROAD
A254
CHAPEL HILL CL
PAYTON CL
ELMLEY WAY
DANE COURT ROAD
SACKETTS HILL
LANE
SHALLOWS ROAD
WESTWOOD INDUSTRIAL ESTATE
STRASBOURG ST
CONTINENTAL APP
ENTERPRISE ROAD
CHANNEL RD
GOODWIN PARK
Nursery
Sacketts Hill Farm
WESTWOOD IND EST
NASH ROAD
GORDON RD
CLIVE RD
CROSSWAYS AV
OCIVAN WAY
STAR LANE
SLOE LANE
Westwood
POORHOLE LANE
MARGATE RD
WESTWOOD RETAIL PK
Factories
Playing Field
EAST KENT RETAIL PK
WESTWOOD GATEWAY
NASH RD
MANSTON COURT ROAD
St Georges C of E Foundation School
WEALDHURST PK
DICKENS LODGE
Supermarket
Dane Court Grammar Sch
DANE COURT GS
DANE CT GDNS
TYLER CL
CANTERBURY CL
VICARAGE
WESTWOOD ROAD
HAINE ROAD
MARGATE ROAD
Health Club
Fire Station
Canterbury ChristChurch University College
RUMFIELDS
ASH CL
Fairfield
WESTWOOD CROSS SHOPPING MALL
Superstore
MILLENNIUM WAY
THANET REACH BSNS PK
SYCAMORE CL
ALMOND CL
SILVERS
THE MAPLES
MARINERS LEA
LEAS GRN
THE HAWTHORNS
BEECH DRIVE
CHESTNUT
LARCH CL
WILLOW AV
YEW TREE DR
Hotel
BROADSTAIRS RETAIL PK
THE SILVERS
THE PINES
PEAR TREE CL
HOLLY CL
BIRCH CL
THE FRANK WALTERS BSNS PK
Bromstone Primary Sch
Cinema
ANTOLIN WAY
ANTOLIN WY
P.H.
Amb Sta
NEW HAINE ROAD
HOLMES WY
Haine Farm
Bus Depot
QUANTOCK GDNS
COXES AV
FAIRLAWN RD
CHERRY GDNS
ANSON CL
HORNET CL
BLENHEIM CL
PATRICIA WAY
VINCENT CL
COXES LANE
Northwood
ORCHARD CL
CHERRY TREE GDNS
HIGHFIELD RD
WINDMILL AV
MARROSE AV
MENTMORE RD
MENTMORE HO
PYSONS RD IND ESTATE
PYSONS
LYSANDER CL
HOME LEIGH RD
NORTHWOOD
DONNAHAY RD
HOPES LANE
MILLFIELD RD
MILL LA
HIGHBURY GDNS
HIGHFIELD CL
THE NOOK
NEWLANDS LA
Jackey Baker's Recreation Ground
BUXTON RD
CHARLTON CL
VIOLET AV
DRIVE
HELMDON CL
Works
MALLORY CL
ROMILLY GDNS
Northwood Centre
ROAD
FITZROY AV
DOROTHY
GREENFIELD ROAD
CLEMENTS
Dame Janet Community Infant & Junior Schools
NEWINGTON ROAD
ROMAN
WINIFRED ROAD
NIXON AVENUE
Newlands Farm
West Dumpton
A256
The Marlowe Academy
DORSET CT
DEVON CT
NORTH CT
ALLENBY
SOUTH CT
ASHLEY
GWYN RD
Whitehall
MARTINS CL
LAWLEY CL
Ellington School for Girls
STIRLING WAY
DURBAN CL
ROCKSTONE
KIMBERLEY
HAMILTON CL
MELBOURNE AV
CONYNGHAM
KINGSTON
B2014
COLEMAN

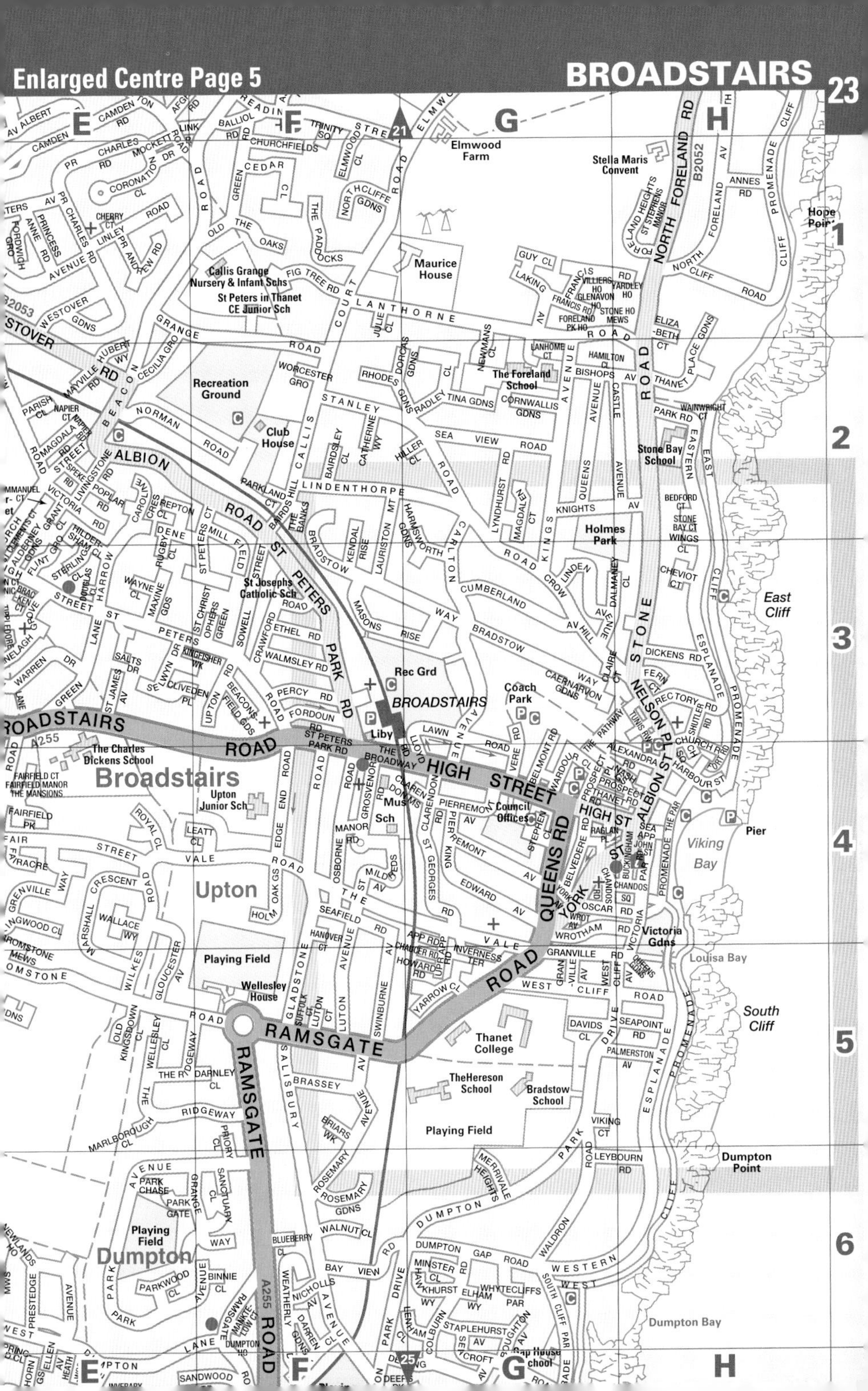
Broadstairs
Upton
Dumpton
Elmwood Farm
Stella Maris Convent
Maurice House
Callis Grange Nursery & Infant Schs
St Peters in Thanet CE Junior Sch
Recreation Ground
Club House
The Foreland School
Stone Bay School
Holmes Park
East Cliff
St Josephs Catholic Sch
Rec Grd
BROADSTAIRS
Coach Park
Liby
The Charles Dickens School
Upton Junior Sch
Council Offices
Mus
Sch
Viking Bay
Pier
Victoria Gdns
Louisa Bay
South Cliff
Playing Field
Wellesley House
Thanet College
TheHereson School
Bradstow School
Dumpton Point
Dumpton Bay
Hope Point
BROADSTAIRS ROAD
HIGH STREET
QUEENS RD
RAMSGATE ROAD
ALBION ROAD
ST PETERS PARK RD
NORTH FORELAND RD
STONE ROAD
LANTHORNE ROAD
WESTERN ESPLANADE
DUMPTON PARK DRIVE
B2052
B2053
A255
E
F
G
H
1
2
3
4
5
6
21
25

A
B
C
D
1
2
3
4
5
6
22
26
Whitehall
Newington
Nethercourt
St. Lawrence
Chilton
Pegwell
Ramsgate
Staner Hill
Hollins Bottom
Spratling Court Farm
Spratling Street Farm
Little Cliffsend Farm
The Marlowe Academy
Haine Ind Est
Community Centre
Newington Community Primary School
Playing Field
Superstore
Filling Station
Factory
Old Timber Yard Ind Est
St Laurence-in-Thanet CE Junior Sch
St Lawrence Ind Est
Rail Maintenance Facility
Warre Rec Grnd
Swimming Pool
Clinic
Club
Games Court
Ellington Schools
Camping Site
Nethercourt Park
Nethercourt Circus
Sports Ground
Chilton Primary Sch
Christchurch C of E Junior Sch
Court Stairs Ldg Nursery Sch
Caravan Park
Court Stairs Park
Miniature Golf Course
Art Gallery
Bowling Green
Croquet Lawn
Paddling Pool
West Cliff
Pegwell Bay
Long Ship 'Hugin'
Haine Road
Manston Road
Canterbury Road East
London Road
Newington Road
Margate Road
Nethercourt Hl
High Street St Lawrence
Royal Harbour Ap
Chalk Hill
Spratling Street
Spratling La
Royal Esplanade
A256
A253
A254
B2014
B2050

E
F
G
H
1
2
3
4
5
6
Newlands Farm
West Dumpton
Dumpton
Playing Field
Ellington School for Girls
Playing Field
Newlands Primary School
Newlands Childrens Centre
Playing Field
Coll
St Lawrence College
DUMPTON PARK
Ramsgate Cemetery
St Lawrence Cemetery
Football Ground
Playing Field
Holy Trinity C of E Primary Sch
Gap House School
Games Centre
King George VI Memorial Park
East Cliff
St Ethelberts Catholic Prim Sch
Medical Centre
Winterstoke Gardens
Chatham House Boys Grammar Sch
Sports Centre
Sch
Coach Sta
Liby
Fire Sta
Sch
Sch
Yacht Marina
Basin
Bascule Bridge
ROYAL HARBOUR
Royal Victoria Pavilion
Ramsgate
Ramsgate Sands
Marina
Lifeboat Station
Lighthouse
East Pier
West Pier
Abbey
Mus
College
Linkspen Bridges
Western Ferry Terminal
Beacon
A255
A254
A253
HERESON ROAD
BOUNDARY ROAD
RAMSGATE ROAD
DUMPTON PARK DRIVE
VICTORIA ROAD
WELLINGTON CRES
ROYAL PARADE
PARAGON
ST AUGUSTINES RD
MADEIRA WALK
HARBOUR PAR
UNDERCLIFF
WINTERSTOKE
MARINA ESPLANADE
ST LUKES AV
ST CHRISTOPHERS MWS
COLLEGE RD
WEST DUMPTON LANE
SHERWOOD GDNS
MONTEFIORE AV
CLIFFSIDE DRIVE
SOUTH CLIFF PARADE

MANSTON

CLIFFS END

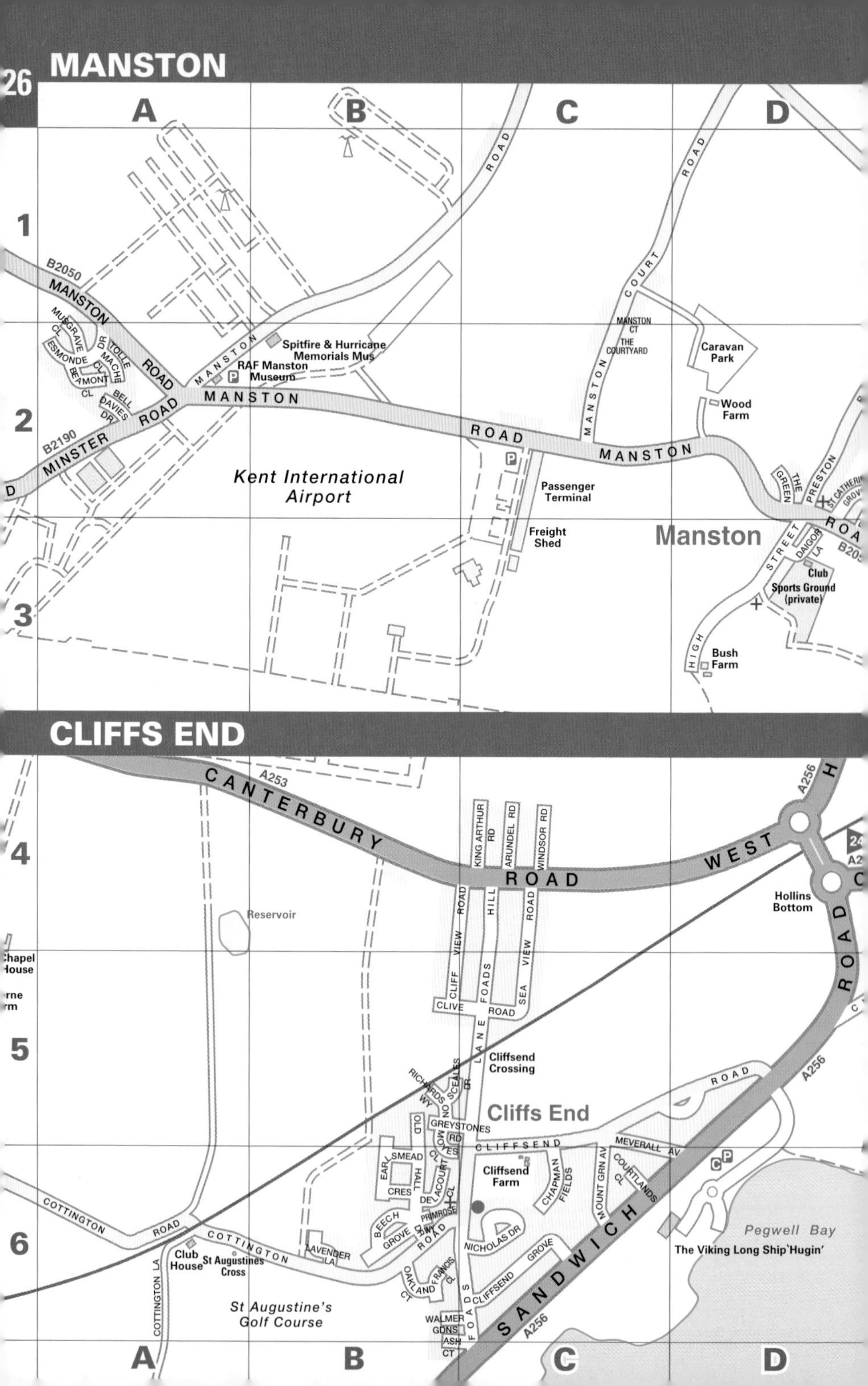

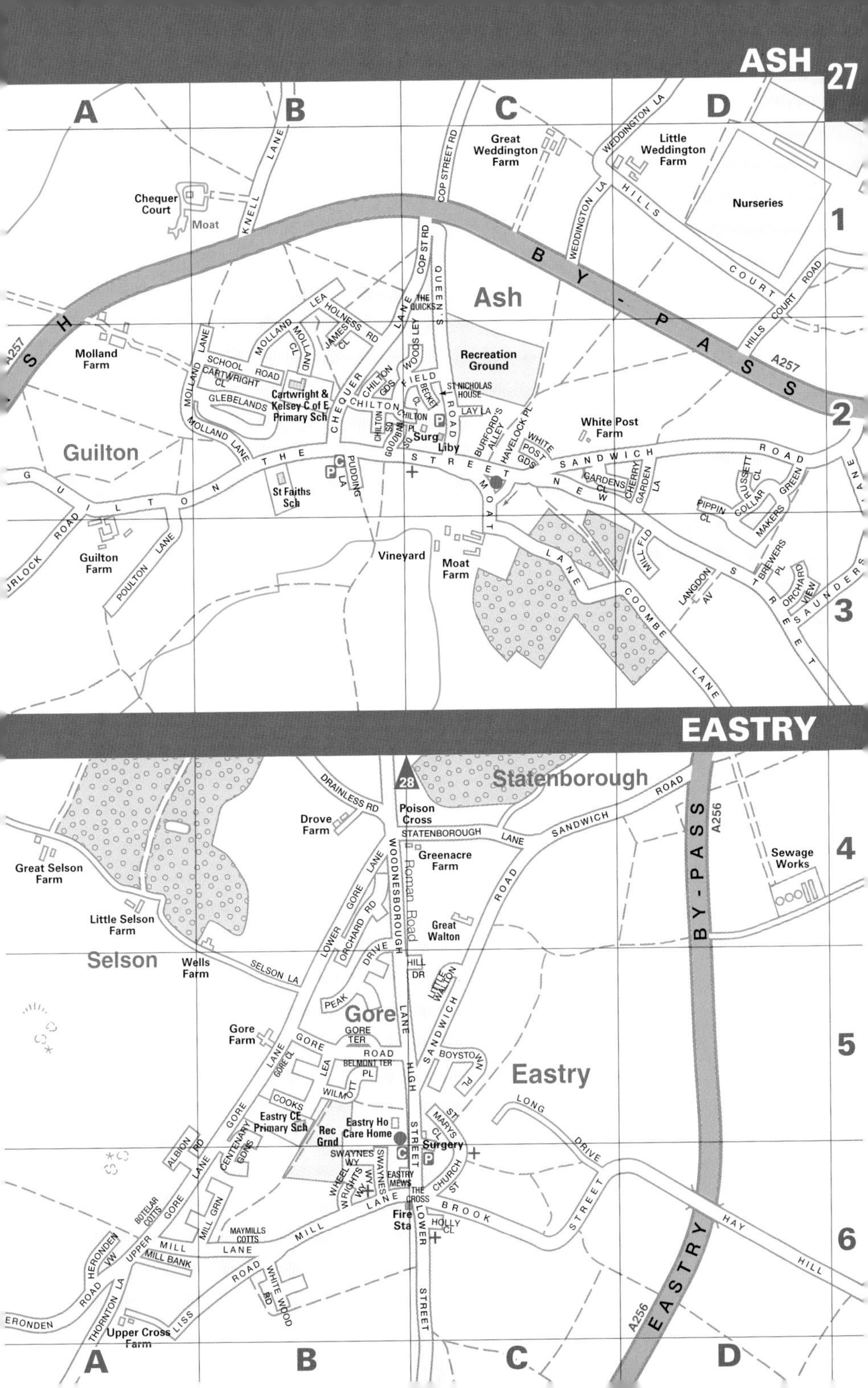
ASH
27
A
B
C
D
Great Weddington Farm
Little Weddington Farm
Nurseries
Chequer Court
Moat
KNELL LANE
COP STREET RD
WEDDINGTON LA
HILLS COURT ROAD
ASH BY-PASS
A257
Ash
Molland Farm
Recreation Ground
THE QUICKS
HOLNESS RD
LEA
MOLLAND LANE
MOLLAND CL
JAMES CL
SCHOOL ROAD
CARTWRIGHT CL
GLEBELANDS
Cartwright & Kelsey C of E Primary Sch
CHEQUER LANE
CHILTON GDS
CHILTON SQ
CHILTON PL
GOODBAN SQ
WOODS LEY
QUEEN'S ROAD
FIELD
BECKET CL
ST NICHOLAS HOUSE
LAY LA
BURFORD'S ALLEY
HAVELOCK PL
WHITE POST GDS
White Post Farm
Surg
Liby
Guilton
THE STREET
GUILTON
PUDDING LA
St Faiths Sch
MOAT
SANDWICH ROAD
NEW ST
GARDENS CL
CHERRY GARDEN LA
RUSSETT CL
PIPPIN CL
COLLAR MAKERS GREEN
GUILTON ROAD
Guilton Farm
POULTON LANE
Vineyard
Moat Farm
LANE
MILL FLD
COOMBE LANE
LANGDON AV
BREWERS PL
ORCHARD VIEW
SAUNDERS
STREET
1
2
3
EASTRY
28
Statenborough
DRAINLESS RD
Drove Farm
Poison Cross
STATENBOROUGH LANE
SANDWICH ROAD
BY-PASS
A256
Greenacre Farm
Sewage Works
Great Selson Farm
Little Selson Farm
WOODNESBOROUGH LANE
Roman Road
GORE LANE
LOWER
ORCHARD RD
DRIVE
Great Walton
ROAD
HILL DR
LITTLE WALTON
Selson
Wells Farm
SELSON LA
PEAK
Gore
SANDWICH
Gore Farm
GORE
GORE TER
ROAD
BOYSTOWN PL
Eastry
GORE CL
LEA
BELMONT TER
PL
WILMOTT
HIGH STREET
LONG DRIVE
COOKS
Eastry CE Primary Sch
Eastry Ho Care Home
ST MARYS CL
Rec Grnd
Surgery
ALBION RD
CENTENARY GDNS
SWAYNES WY
SWAYNES WY
EASTRY MEWS
CHURCH ST
WHEEL WRIGHTS WY
THE CROSS
BROOK
STREET
HAY HILL
BOTELAR COTTS
MILL GRN
LANE
Fire Sta
HOLLY CL
LOWER STREET
MAYMILLS COTTS
MILL LANE
HERONDEN VW
UPPER MILL LANE
MILL BANK
ROAD
WHITE WOOD RD
EASTRY
THORNTON LA
HERONDEN
Upper Cross Farm
LISS
4
5
6

A
B
C
D
1
2
3
4
5
6
SANDWICH ROAD
A257
A256
North Poulders
White Mill Folk Museum
IND EST
THE CAUSEWAY
ASH ROAD
SANDWICH BY-PASS
South Poulders
EACH END COTTS
Each End
Each End House
EAST ST
ST STREET
POULDERS ROAD
SUNNYSIDE GS
White Cliffs Country Trail
POULDERS GDNS
Marshborough Farm
Chestnut Farm
Vine Farm
Marshborough
PARSONAGE FARM RD
Parsonage Farm
MARSHBOROUGH ROAD
CLAREMONT TER
WOODNESBOROUGH ROAD
Poulders Gardens
MELVILLE LEA
SANDWICH
THE STREET
PARK TER
HILL ROAD
BEACON LANE
FROST COTTS
WOODLAND WY
Woodnesborough House
OAK HILL
FIR TREE HILL
CHURCH FM WY
OAST COTTS
GROVE MANOR
MANOR BARNS
CHURCH STREET
ST MARYS CL
Churchgate Farm
FOXBOROUGH CL
THE BUNGALOWS
FOXBOROUGH HILL
Woodnesborough
Nurseries
Water Garden Centre
SANDWICH ROAD
Buckland Farm
JOHNS GREEN
Foxborough Farm
Hill Cross Farm
DRAINLESS ROAD
Highborough Hill
FELDERLAND
27

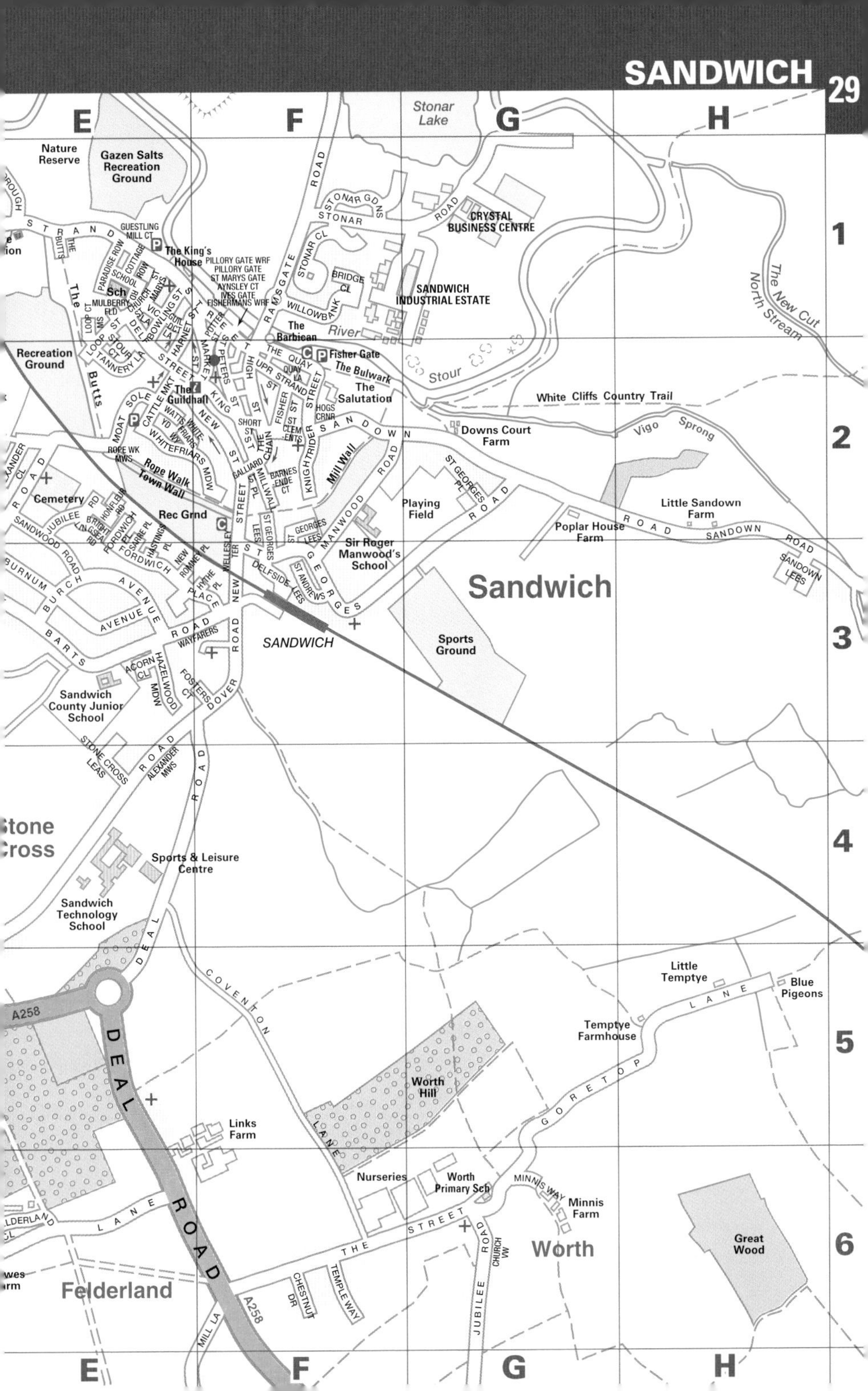
Stonar Lake
Nature Reserve
Gazen Salts Recreation Ground
The King's House
CRYSTAL BUSINESS CENTRE
SANDWICH INDUSTRIAL ESTATE
The Barbican
Fisher Gate
The Bulwark
The Salutation
River Stour
The New Cut
North Stream
White Cliffs Country Trail
Downs Court Farm
Vigo Sprong
Recreation Ground
The Guildhall
Rope Walk
Town Wall
Rec Grnd
Cemetery
Mill Wall
Playing Field
Sir Roger Manwood's School
Poplar House Farm
Little Sandown Farm
Sandwich
SANDWICH
Sports Ground
Sandwich County Junior School
Stone Cross
Sports & Leisure Centre
Sandwich Technology School
Little Temptye
Blue Pigeons
Temptye Farmhouse
Worth Hill
Links Farm
Nurseries
Worth Primary Sch
Minnis Farm
Worth
Great Wood
Felderland
DEAL ROAD
A258
COVENTON LANE
GORETOP LANE
THE STREET
SANDOWN ROAD
RAMSGATE ROAD
STONAR

A
B
C
D
1
2
3
4
5
6
A290
BLEAN
BROADLANDS IND EST
THE GAP
TRUEMAN CL
BADGERS CL
CHAPEL
LANE
BOURNE LODGE CL
Old Walnut Tree Farm
SCHOOL LANE
CHESTNUT AV
FISHER CT
WOODVILLE
Reservoir (Covered)
WESTFIELD
Hall
Rec Grd
TYLER HILL RD
TYLER HILL ROAD
THE GREEN
COMMON
Blean
MOUNT PLEASANT
VICARAGE LA
St. Cosmos & St. Damian in the Blean
Hothe Court Farm
FLEETS
SUNNYMEAD
Hillside Farm
Luckett's Farm
Stray Lees Farm
Hare & Hounds P.H.
BLEAN HILL TILE KILN HILL WHITSTABLE ROAD ST THOMAS HILL
UNIVERSITY OF KENT AT CANTERBURY
Playing Field
Pav
Blean Cty Prim Sch
PARK WOOD ROAD
PURCHAS CT
LYPEATT CT
Canterbury Bsns Sch
R&D Centre
Laboratories
Sports Centre
BOSSENDEN CT
NICKLE CT
STOCK CT
KEMSDALE CT
ELLENDEN CT
BISHOPDEN CT
THORNDEN CT
FARTHINGS CT
GRIMSHILL CT
CLOWES CT
MARLEY CT
HOMESTALL CT
TUDOR CT
DENSTEAD CT
WILLOWS CT
WOODLAND WY
BROTHERHOOD CL
Keynes College
Church Wood
MOAT LANE
Playing Fields
PARK OAKS
PARK ROAD
COMMON ROAD
HIGHFIELD CL
GILES
NEW ROAD
Kent College
ROUGH COMMON ROAD
RAVENSCOURT RD
LOVELL ROAD
FIRTREE CL
ROSS GDNS
ROSS GARDENS
MAPLE HO
Rough Common
MAPLE CL
STOCKWOOD CHASE
NEALS PLACE ROAD
THE CLOSE
Beverley Farm
St Edmunds School
UNIVERSITY
Chaucer College
GLEN IRIS AVENUE
GLEN IRIS CL
Stock Wood
CHURCH WOOD CL
SYDNEY COOPER CL
Hall
Sports Ground
CHERRY AV
RICHMOND GDNS
CHERRY GARDEN RD
MEADOW RD
HILLVIEW ROAD
HILLSIDE AVENUE
CHERRY DR
CHERRY DRIVE
GARDEN CL
ROUGH
ST MICHAELS CL
The Grove
CLIFTON GDNS
HARCOURT DR
Cemetery
PALM
HALL PLACE ENTERPRISE CENTRE
34
CEDARVIEW
AVENUE
Dav Wo

Honey Wood
Great Hall Wood
Barton Wood
Tyler Hill
Little Hall Wood
Brickhouse Wood
Little Hall Farm
Hales Place
Barton Down
Darwin College
Cornwallis Building
Gulbenkian Theatre
Templeman Library
Tyler Court
Rutherford College
Eliot College
The Archbishop's School
St Stephens Junior School
Playing Field
Rec Grd
St. Stephen's
Vauxhall Lakes
Superstores
Works
Kingsmead Coach Park
Depot
Leisure Centre
Rec Centre
Tennis Courts
Supermarket
Council Offices
CANTERBURY HILL
ST STEPHENS HILL
HACKINGTON RD
SUMMER LANE
TYLER HILL
DOWNS ROAD
HALES DRIVE
BROAD OAK ROAD
STURRY ROAD
A28
32
35

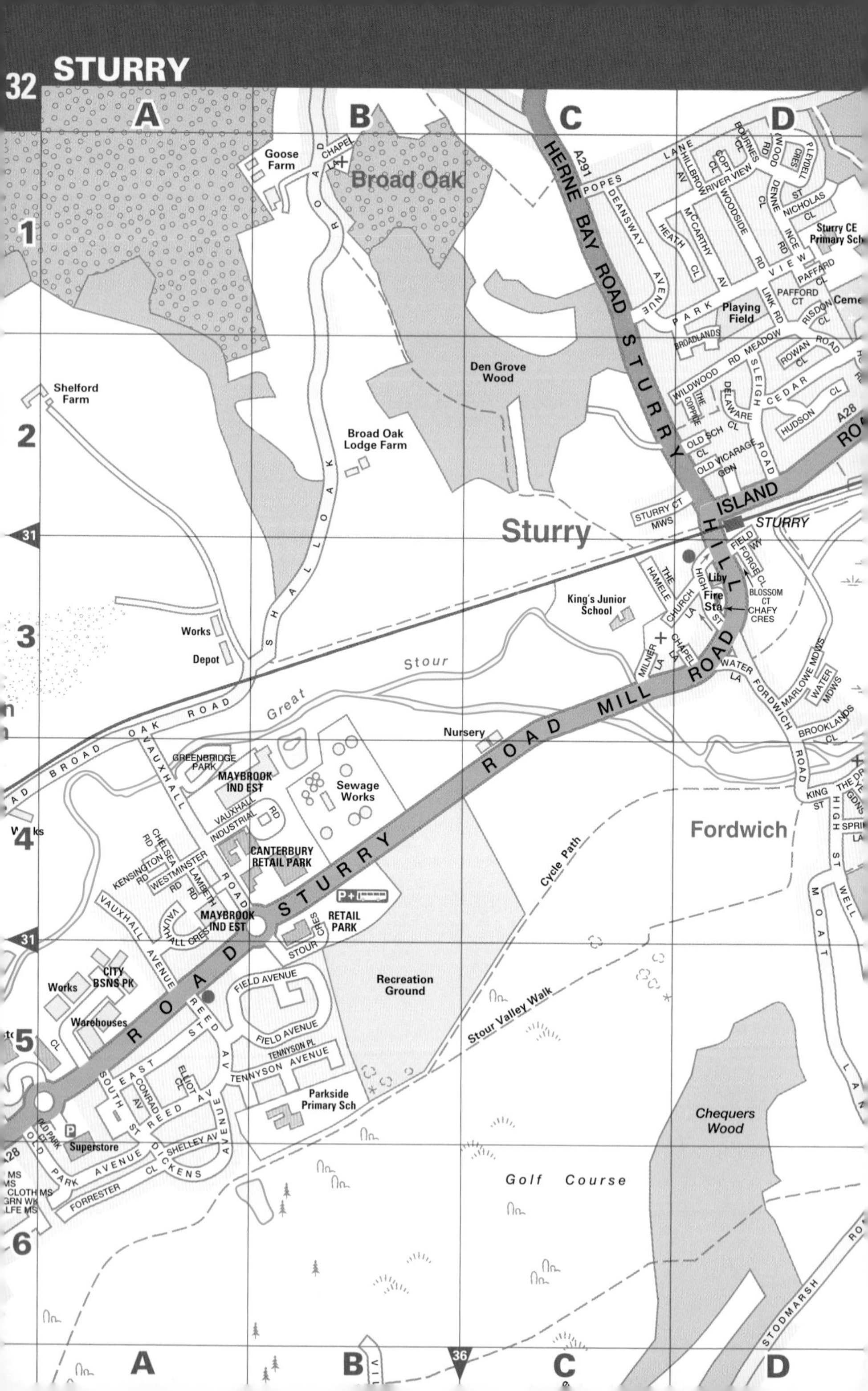

A
B
C
D
1
2
3
4
5
6
Goose Farm
Broad Oak
Shelford Farm
Broad Oak Lodge Farm
Den Grove Wood
Sturry
Works
Depot
King's Junior School
Great Stour
Nursery
Sewage Works
MAYBROOK IND EST
CANTERBURY RETAIL PARK
RETAIL PARK
Recreation Ground
CITY BSNS PK
Works
Warehouses
Superstore
Parkside Primary Sch
Fordwich
Cycle Path
Stour Valley Walk
Golf Course
Chequers Wood
Playing Field
Sturry CE Primary Sch
HERNE BAY ROAD
STURRY ROAD
STURRY HILL
MILL ROAD
ISLAND
A291
A28
SHALLOAK ROAD
BROAD OAK ROAD
VAUXHALL AVENUE
FIELD AVENUE
TENNYSON AVENUE
STODMARSH
36
31

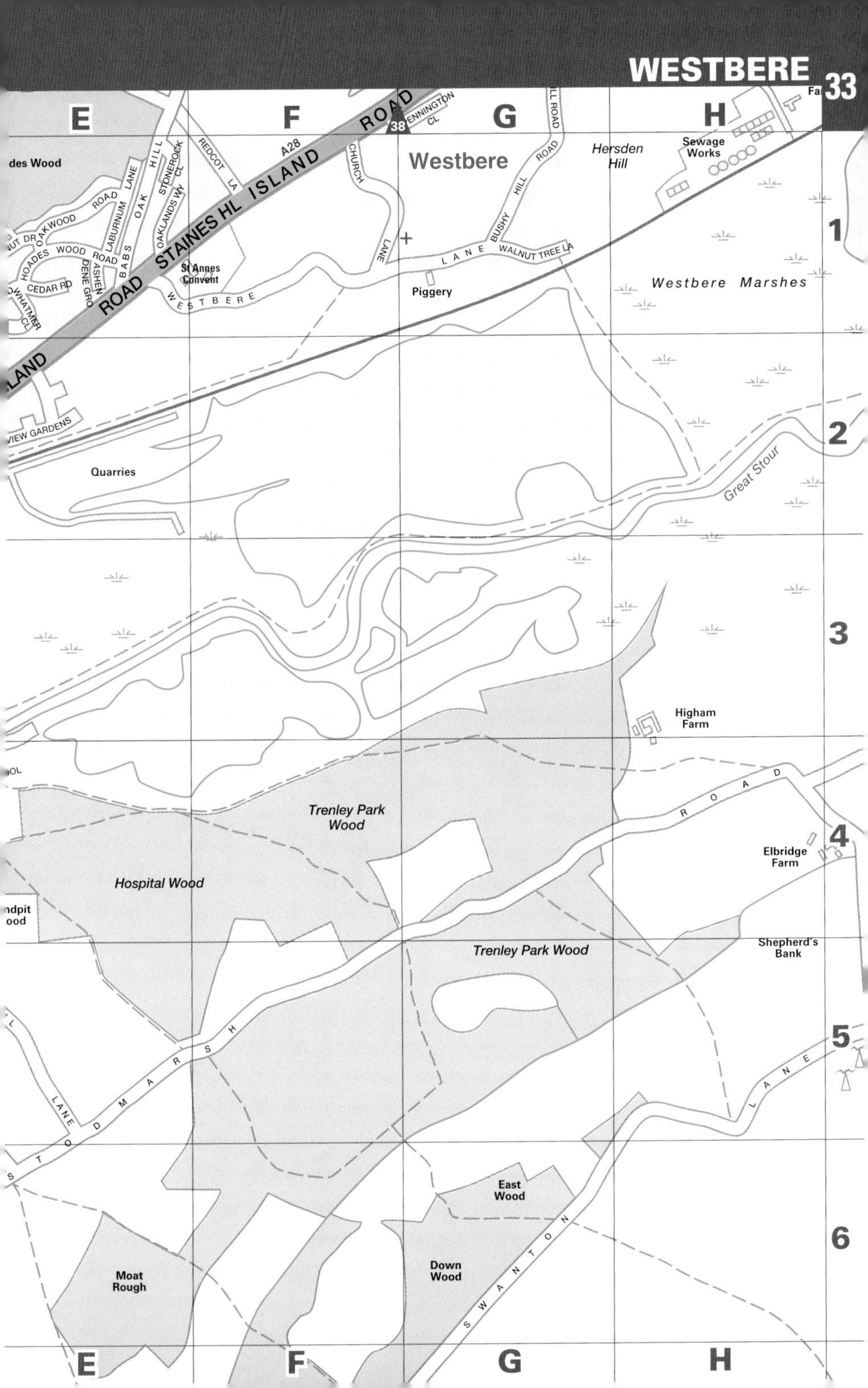
E
F
G
H
des Wood
A28
ROAD
ISLAND
STAINES HL
ROAD
LAND
38
ENNINGTON CL
REDCOT LA
CHURCH LANE
Westbere
HILL ROAD
BUSHY HILL ROAD
Hersden Hill
Sewage Works
OAKWOOD
ROAD
LABURNUM LANE
OAK HILL
STONEROCK CL
OAKLANDS WY
BABS
HOADES WOOD ROAD
DENE GRO
ASHEN
CEDAR RD
WHATMER CL
St Annes Convent
WESTBERE LANE
WALNUT TREE LA
Piggery
Westbere Marshes
VIEW GARDENS
Quarries
Great Stour
Higham Farm
Trenley Park Wood
Hospital Wood
ROAD
Elbridge Farm
Shepherd's Bank
Trenley Park Wood
STODMARSH
LANE
LANE
East Wood
Down Wood
Moat Rough
SWANTON
1
2
3
4
5
6

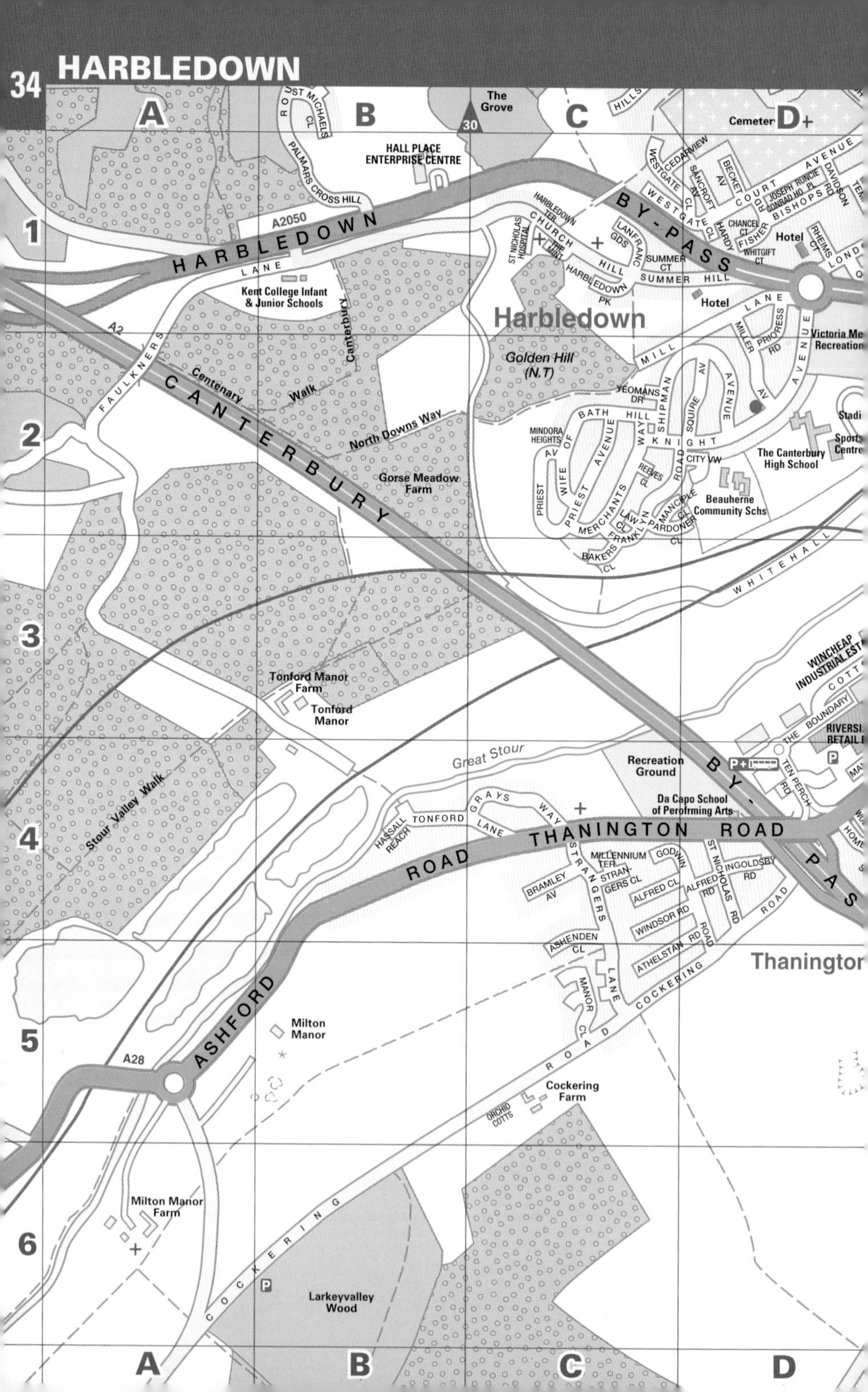

The Grove
30
HALL PLACE ENTERPRISE CENTRE
ST MICHAELS CL
PALMARS CROSS HILL
A2050
HARBLEDOWN BY-PASS
LANE
Kent College Infant & Junior Schools
A2
FAULKNERS
Centenary Walk
Canterbury
CANTERBURY
North Downs Way
Gorse Meadow Farm
Tonford Manor Farm
Tonford Manor
Stour Valley Walk
Great Stour
TONFORD LANE
HASSALL REACH
GRAYS WAY
ASHFORD ROAD
A28
THANINGTON ROAD
Recreation Ground
Da Capo School of Perofrming Arts
Milton Manor
Cockering Farm
ORCHID COTTS
COCKERING ROAD
Milton Manor Farm
Larkeyvalley Wood
Harbledown
Golden Hill (N.T)
HARBLEDOWN TER
CHURCH HILL
THE MINT
ST NICHOLAS HOSPITAL
LANFRANC GDS
HARBLEDOWN PK
SUMMER CT
SUMMER HILL
Hotel
MILL LANE
MILLER AV
PRIORESS RD
Victoria Me Recreation
AVENUE
YEOMANS DR
BATH HILL
MINDORA HEIGHTS
WIFE OF BATH
PRIEST AV
AVENUE
SHIPMAN AV
SQUIRE AV
WAY
KNIGHT AVENUE
CITY VW
REEVES CL
ROAD
MERCHANTS CL
LAWN
FRANKLYN
MANCIPLE CL
PARDONER CL
BAKERS CL
Beauherne Community Schs
The Canterbury High School
Stadi
Sports Centre
WHITEHALL
WESTGATE CL
CEDARVIEW
SANCROFT AV
BECKET AV
WESTGATE
HARDY
FISHER RD
CHANCEL CT
WHITGIFT CT
COURT AVENUE
JOSEPH RUNCIE CONRAD HO PL
BISHOPS
DAVIDSON RD
RHEIMS CT
Hotel
Cemetery
HILLS
WINCHEAP INDUSTRIAL EST
COTT
THE BOUNDARY
RIVERSI RETAIL
TEN PERCH RD
MILLENNIUM TER
STRANGERS CL
STRANGERS LANE
BRAMLEY AV
GODWIN
ALFRED CL
ALFRED RD
ST NICHOLAS RD
INGOLDSBY RD
WINDSOR RD
ROAD
ATHELSTAN RD
ASHENDEN CL
MANOR CL
Thanington
A B C D
1 2 3 4 5 6

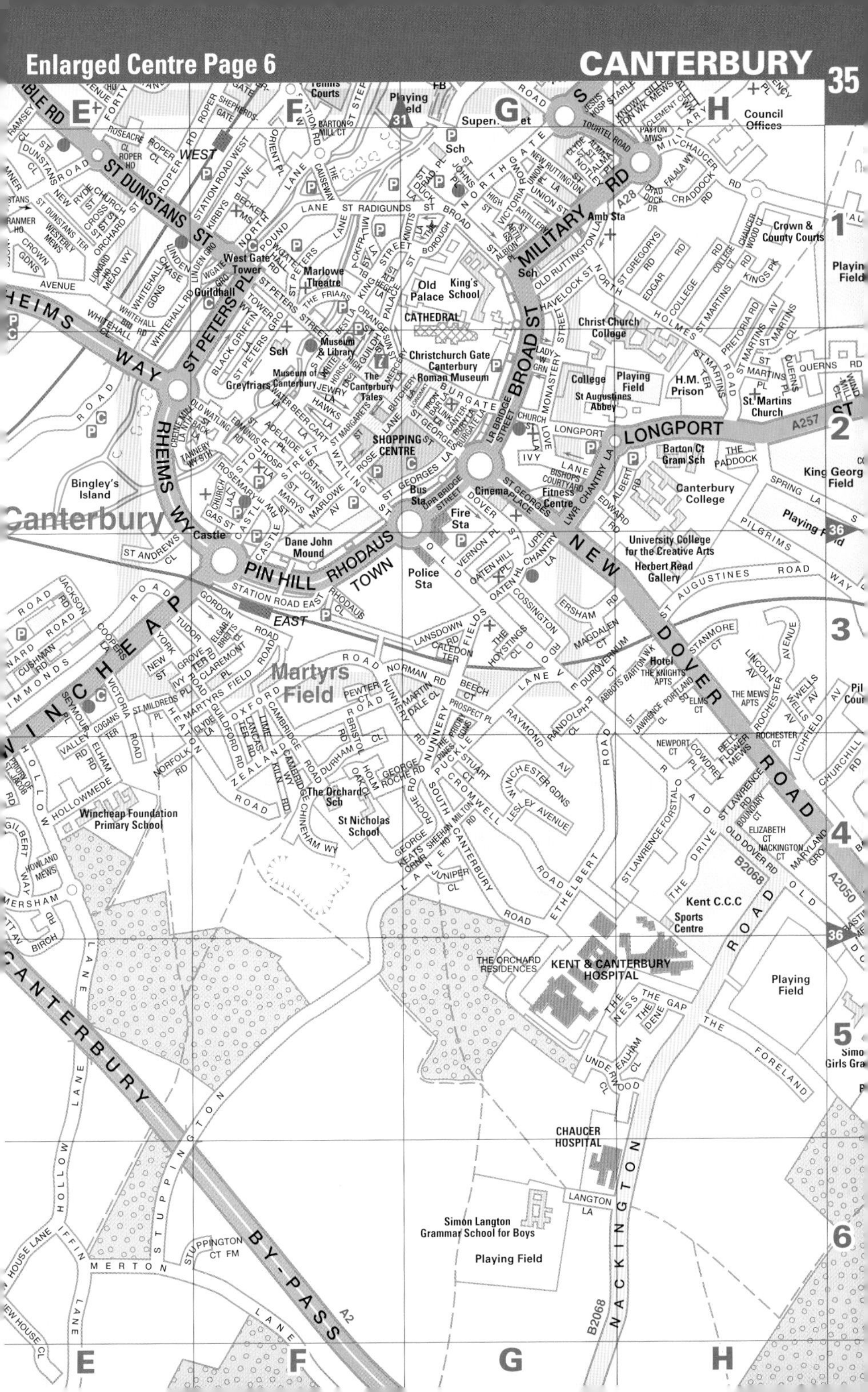
E
F
G
H
1
2
3
4
5
6
31
36
ST DUNSTANS ST
WEST
STATION ROAD WEST
ROPER RD
ROSEACRE CL
ROPER CL
NEW RUTHINGTON
ST DUNSTANS TER
ORCHARD ST
WHITEHALL RD
WHITEHALL GDNS
WHITEHALL CHASE
LINDEN GRO
RHEIMS WAY
ST PETERS PL
ST PETERS ST
ST PETERS LA
ST PETERS GRO
BLACK GRIFFIN LA
NORTH LA
POUND LA
West Gate Tower
Guildhall
Marlowe Theatre
THE FRIARS
Sch
Museum & Library
Greyfriars
Museum of Canterbury
The Canterbury Tales
Christchurch Gate
Canterbury Roman Museum
CATHEDRAL
Old Palace
King's School
ST RADIGUNDS ST
NORTHGATE
BROAD ST
MILITARY RD
Amb Sta
Council Offices
Crown & County Courts
Christ Church College
College
Playing Field
St Augustines Abbey
H.M. Prison
St. Martins Church
ST MARTINS RD
ST MARTINS AV
QUERNS RD
LONGPORT
A257
Barton Ct Gram Sch
THE PADDOCK
King George Field
Canterbury College
SPRING LA
PILGRIMS WAY
University College for the Creative Arts
Herbert Read Gallery
ST AUGUSTINES ROAD
SHOPPING CENTRE
Bus Sta
Cinema
Fitness Centre
Fire Sta
Police Sta
ST GEORGES PLACE
ST GEORGES LA
UPR BRIDGE STREET
LR BRIDGE STREET
BURGATE
NEW DOVER ROAD
OLD DOVER RD
RHODAUS TOWN
PIN HILL
Dane John Mound
Castle
CASTLE ST
Canterbury
Bingley's Island
ST ANDREWS CL
STATION ROAD EAST
EAST
WINCHEAP
Martyrs Field
MARTYRS FIELD ROAD
NUNNERY FIELDS
OXFORD RD
CAMBRIDGE RD
The Orchard Sch
St Nicholas School
CHINEHAM WY
Wincheap Foundation Primary School
HOLLOWMEDE
HOLLOW LANE
CANTERBURY BY-PASS
A2
STUPPINGTON LA
STUPPINGTON CT FM
MERTON LANE
RAYMOND AV
WINCHESTER GDNS
LESLEY AVENUE
CROMWELL RD
SOUTH CANTERBURY ROAD
ETHELBERT ROAD
ST LAWRENCE FORSTAL
THE DRIVE
Kent C.C.C Sports Centre
B2068
A2050
THE ORCHARD RESIDENCES
KENT & CANTERBURY HOSPITAL
THE GAP
THE FORELAND
Playing Field
CHAUCER HOSPITAL
LANGTON LA
Simon Langton Grammar School for Boys
Playing Field
NACKINGTON ROAD
MILITARY RD
CHAUCER RD
A28
HAVELOCK ST
NORTH HOLMES RD
ST GREGORYS RD
EDGAR RD
COLLEGE RD
PRETORIA RD
LOVE LA
MONASTERY ST
LWR CHANTRY LA
CHANTRY LA
OATEN HILL
DOVER ST
ERSHAM RD
DUROVERNUM CT
Hotel
ROCHESTER AV
LICHFIELD AV
STANMORE CT
Simon Langton Girls Grammar

A
B
C
D
32
37
35
1
2
3
4
5
6
Golf Course
Scotland Hills
TRENLEY DR
Christ Church College
Post Graduate Centre
Sports Ground
Hockey Pitch
Tennis Courts
Hockey Pitch
Club
Club House
STODMARSH ROAD
CHAUCER ROAD
Playing Field
SOBRAON WY
PILCKEM CL
SOMME CT
ALBUHERA SQ
VILLIERS ROAD
TUNIS CT
CAMBRAI CT
AISNE DR
BURMA CRES
YPRES CT
ST JULIEN AV
BLENHEIM AV
DOURO CL
SEVASTOPOL PL
SANGRO PL
TALAVERA ROAD
WEMYSS WY
St Martins
Howe Barracks
DONEGAL RD
QUERNS RD
WINDMILL CL
ST MARTINS HILL LITTLEBOURNE ROAD
AVON CL
WINDMILL RD
ST. MARTINS HOSPITAL
ELISONS WK
CONFERENCE WK
WARWICK RD
SOMERSET RD
HERTFORD CT
COLLARD HO
KENT AVENUE
DEVON RD
King George's Field
NONSUCH CL
LAXTON WY
STURMER CL
RUSSETT RD
FIESTA WK
DISCOVERY WK
WINSTON CL
ESSEX RD
SUFFOLK RD
RUTLAND CL
Camping & Caravan Site
BEKESBOURNE LANE
SUSSEX AVENUE
CORNWALL GDNS
CUMBERLAND AV
ORCHARD FLATS
HAMPSHIRE RD
DORSET RD
SURREY RD
SPRING LANE
PILGRIMS WAY
Chaucer Technology College.
Little Barton Farm
WORCESTER LA
Hoath Farm
Playing Field
BYRON CL
DRYDEN CL
CHAUCER CL
Pilgrims Way County Prim Sch
LICHFIELD AV
CHURCHILL RD
MOUNT ROAD
BARTON ROAD
MILTON CL
BARTON RD
COBHAM CL
BARTON BUSINESS PK
Palmsted Wood
North Downs Ways
Appledown Way
A2050
NEW DOVER ROAD
BASTIEN MEWS
OLD DOVER ROAD
Simon Langton Girls Grammar School
Playing Field
St Anselms Catholic Sch
Haystack Wood
Hode Farm
Milestone

A
B
C
D
36
1
2
3
4
5
6
Haystack Wood
Bekesbourne Farm
OAKLEIGH LANE
BEKESBOURNE LANE
Bekesbourne Hill
YEW TREE COTTS
NEWPORT COTTS
HOWLETTS OAST
BEKESBOURNE
HILLSIDE COTTS
HOLLYTREE COTTS
Hode Farm
SCHOOL LANE
ROAD
CRANMER CL
ASPINALL CL
BIFRONS RD
STATION
BIFRONS HILL
Patrixbourne
Recreation Ground
THE STREET
BIFRONS GDNS
ST MARYS RD
Fords
KEEPERS HILL
A2
BRIDGE
Bifron's Park
BEKESBOURNE RD
TOWN HILL
Elham Valley Way
LANE
CONYNGHAM
THE NEW CL
Bridge & Patrixbourne C of E Primary Sch
Nail Bourne
PATRIXBOURNE ROAD
Anglo-Saxon Burial Ground
HIGH
AUNT BETSYS HILL
DERING CL
DERING ROAD
FILMER RD
THE CLOSE
MOUNT CHARLES WK
CHURCHILL CL
UNION
SAXON RD
Rec Grnd
Surgery
RIVERSIDE CL
BIRONS PATH
RIVERSIDE MS
Great Pett Farm
PETT HILL
MILL TER
BOURNE VIEW
MILL
WESTERN AV
FORD CL
WINDMILL
GREEN CT
BRIDGEFORD WY
BREWERY LA
STREET
Bridge
BY-PASS
Ford
LANE
Brickfield Farm
MEADOW CL
BEECH HILL
BRIDGE
BOURNE PARK ROAD
BRIDGE DOWN
HIGHAM CT COTTS
HIGHAM LA
Higham Park
Tumuli
Bourne Park
HIGHAM
PIPPIN AV
HILL
Cold Stores
Warren Plantation
A2

LITTLEBOURNE
A
B
C
D
1
2
3
Ickham
Ickham Court Farm
Treasury Farm
Ickham Hall
White Bridge
Reynolds Place
RIVERSIDE COTTS
Littlebourne Water Mill
CHERRY ORCHARD
CHERRY ORCH MEWS
LITTLEBOURNE CT
BUILDERS SQ
ST VINCENTS CL
THE ELDERS
COURT MEADOWS
COURT HILL
PINESIDE RD
HILLCREST RD
EVENHILL RD
NEWING CL
LIST MDWS
Littlebourne C of E Primary Sch
CHURCH ROAD
NARGATE CL
ELMLEIGH RD
NARGATE STREET
Little Stour
TREASURY VW
SCHOOL LANE
CHERVILLE LANE
WICKHAM LA
DRILL LANE
THE STREET
A257
THE HILL
HIGH STREET
YEW TREE CT
JUBILEE ROAD
Rec Grnd
Hall
ELLEN CT
LITTLE CT
SCHOOL PATH
ROSE ACRE RD
ORCHARD CL
THE MALTINGS
THE GREEN
Littlebourne
LANE THE
BEKESBOURNE
P
HERSDEN
4
5
6
Gravel Pit
Joiners Farm
BMX Track
Playground
Bowling Green
Rec Grnd
Hersden Cty Prim Sch
ST ALBANS RD
SUTTON RD
SHAFTESBURY RD
Club
THE FIRS
ASH CRESCENT
THE ELMS
THE OAKS
THE POPLARS
AVENUE
EAST VW
NORTH VW
CHISLET PK COTTS
THE VILLAS
ROAD
CLAREMONT WY
SPARROW WY
THOMAS WAY
CHISLET CL
MINERS WY
LAKEVIEW INTERNATIONAL BUSINESS PARK
STONE WY
CANTERBURY INDUSTRIAL PARK
Hersden
Bredlands Farm
BLACKTHORN
HAZEL CT
MAPLE CT
THE AVENUE
MAPLE GDNS
THE SYCAMORES
LARCH CL
BLACKTHORN RD
ACACIA DR
BREDLANDS LANE
Playing Field
ISLAND ROAD
A28
BUSHY HILL ROAD
Hoplands Farm
Stour Valley Walk
Stodmarsh Valley
Great Stour
Haseden Farm
Sewage Works
33
Hersden
ere

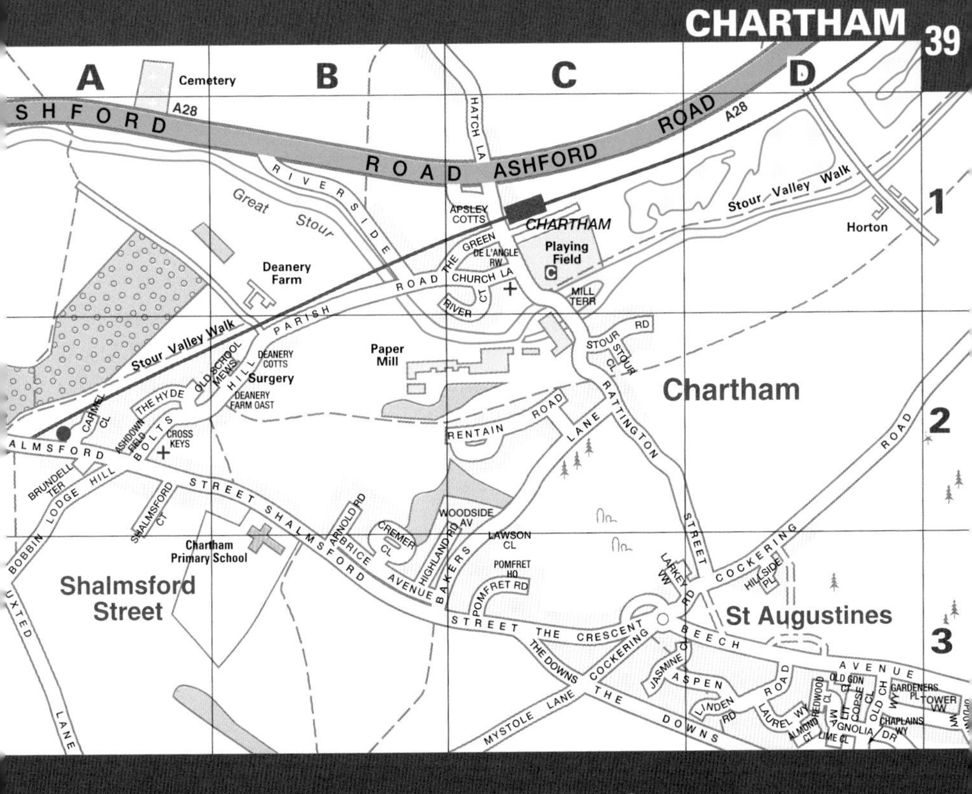

INDEX TO STREETS

with Postcodes

ıe Index includes some
ımes for which there is
sufficient space on the
aps. These names are
dicated by an * and are
llowed by the nearest
djoining thoroughfare.

ɔbey Ct, Westgate-on-Sea
:T8 17 H4
ɔbey Ct,
Vhitstable CT5 9 H1
ɔbey Gate CT11 24 C5
ɔbey Gdns CT2 31 G5
ɔbey Gro,
Minster CT12 15 C6
ɔbey Gro,
Pegwell CT11 24 C5
ɔbey Way CT11 4 D1
ɔbots Barton Walk
:T1 35 G3
ɔbots Hill CT11 4 D2
ɔbots Pl CT1 6 C2
cacia Dr CT3 38 A5
col Hill CT7 17 E6
corn Cl CT13 29 E3
cton Rd CT5 9 F2
da Rd CT1 35 E4
ddington Pl CT11 4 C3
ddington Rd CT9 3 E3
ddington Sq CT9 3 E3
ddington St,
Margate CT9 3 D3
ddington St,
Ramsgate CT11 4 B3
ddiscombe Gdns
:T9 19 G4
ddiscombe Rd
:T9 19 H4

Adelaide Gdns CT11 4 C3
Adelaide Pl CT1 6 B4
Adisham Way CT9 20 B4
Admiralty Walk CT5 8 B5
Adrian Mews CT8 18 A4
Adrian Sq CT8 18 A4
Afghan Rd CT10 21 E6
Airedale Cl CT9 19 H3
Aisne Dr CT1 36 B1
Albany Dr CT6 12 A2
Albert Ct CT11 4 D2
Albert Mews, Margate
CT9 3 E4
Albert Mews, Canterbury
CT1 31 H6
Albert Mws CT11 4 C3
Albert Rd, Broadstairs
CT10 20 D6
Albert Rd, Canterbury
CT1 35 H2
Albert Rd, Margate
CT9 3 A3
Albert Rd, Ramsgate
CT11 25 G3
Albert Row CT11 24 D5
Albert St, Ramsgate
CT11 4 C3
Albert St, Whitstable
CT5 9 E2
Albert Ter CT9 3 C3
Albion Cl CT6 14 D1
Albion Ct CT11 4 D2
Albion Hill CT11 4 D2
Albion Ho CT11 4 E2
Albion La CT6 14 D1
Albion Mews CT11 4 E2
Albion Pl, Canterbury
CT1 6 D2

Albion Pl, Ramsgate
CT11 4 E2
Albion Pl, Margate
CT9 3 D1
Albion Rd, Birchington
CT7 17 E3
Albion Rd, Broadstairs
CT10 23 E2
Albion Rd, Margate
CT9 20 A3
Albion Rd, Ramsgate
CT11 25 G3
Albion Rd, Sandwich
CT13 27 A6
Albion St CT10 5 C3
Albuhera Sq CT1 36 B1
Alderney Gdns
CT10 23 E3
Aldridge Cl CT6 11 G3
Alexander Cl CT13 29 E2
Alexandra Ct CT9 19 E3
Alexandra Homes
CT9 19 F4
Alexandra Rd, Birchington
CT7 17 E5
Alexandra Rd, Broadstairs
CT10 5 C3
Alexandra Rd, Margate
CT9 19 F4
Alexandra Rd, Ramsgate
CT11 25 E3
Alexandra Rd, Whitstable
CT5 9 E4
Alexandra Ter CT9 19 G4
Alexandria Dr CT6 11 G1
Alfred Cl CT1 34 C4
Alfred Ct CT7 17 E4
Alfred Rd, Birchington
CT7 16 B2

Alfred Rd, Canterbury
CT1 34 D4
Alfred Rd, Margate
CT9 20 A4
Alicia Av CT9 18 B4
Alison Cl CT7 17 F2
Alkali Row CT9 3 D2
Alkham Cl CT9 21 E3
All Saints Av CT9 3 A4
All Saints Cl CT5 9 G3
All Saints Ct CT1 6 B3
All Saints Ind Est
CT9 3 B4
All Saints La CT1 6 B3
Allan Rd CT5 8 A5
Alland Grange La
CT12 15 D2
Allen Av CT8 17 G3
Allenby Rd CT12 22 B6
Alliance Rd CT11 4 E2
Alma Pl, Canterbury
CT1 35 G1
Alma Pl, Ramsgate
CT11 4 E1
Alma Rd, Herne Bay
CT6 13 E2
Alma Rd, Margate
CT9 3 E4
Alma Rd, Ramsgate
CT11 25 F3
Alma St CT1 35 G1
Almarina CT8 18 A3
Almond Cl, Broadstairs
CT10 22 C4
Almond Cl, Whitstable
CT5 10 C4
Almond Ct CT4 39 D3
Alpha Rd, Birchington
CT7 17 E3

Alpha Rd, Ramsgate
CT11 4 B2
Alvis Av CT6 11 E2
Amberley Ct CT11 4 F1
Ambleside Pl CT2 31 G6
Amherst Cl CT9 20 C4
Amos Cl CT6 13 E3
Anchor Hill CT9 3 E2
Ancress Cl CT2 31 G4
Anemone Way CT6 14 B2
Angel Ct CT1 6 C3
Anna Pk CT7 16 D2
Anne Cl CT7 17 F3
Anne Gibson Ct
CT11 4 D2
Anne Green Walk
CT1 31 H6
Anne Ho CT9 3 E1
Anne Marie Ct CT6 12 C3
Annes Rd CT10 21 H6
Anns Rd CT11 25 F3
Anson Cl CT10 22 C5
Anthony Cl CT12 24 C2
Anthony Cres CT5 8 C6
Antolin Way CT12 22 A5
Anvil Cl CT7 17 E4
Appledore Cl CT9 20 B4
Applegarth Pk CT5 8 B6
Approach Rd, Broadstairs
CT10 5 A4
Approach Rd, Margate
CT9 20 A3
April Rise, Whitstable
CT5 8 D5
April Rise, Birchington
CT7 16 B2
Apsley Cotts CT4 39 C1
Apsley Ct CT11 4 E1
Archway Rd CT11 4 C2

Arden Rd CT6 13 E5
Argyle Av CT9 18 D4
Argyle Gdns CT9 18 D4
Argyle Rd CT5 9 E3
Argyll Dr CT11 25 F1
Arkley Rd CT6 12 C3
Arklow Sq CT11 4 E1
Arlington Gdns CT9 20 B6
Arlington Sq CT9 3 B3
Armstrong Sq CT6 11 F2
Arnold Rd, Canterbury CT4 39 B3
Arnold Rd, Margate CT9 3 E4
Arolla Rd CT6 13 E3
Arran Mews CT1 31 H6
Arthur Rd, Birchington CT7 16 B3
Arthur Rd, Margate CT9 19 H2
Artillery Gdns CT1 6 D2
Artillery Ho CT1 6 D2
Artillery Rd CT11 4 E1
Artillery St CT1 6 D2
Arundel Rd, Margate CT9 20 A4
Arundel Rd, Ramsgate CT12 26 C4
Ascot Gdns CT8 18 A5
Ash By-Pass CT3 27 A2
Ash Cl, Broadstairs CT10 22 C4
Ash Cl, Herne Bay CT6 12 C6
Ash Cres CT3 38 B5
Ash Lodge CT6 12 C2
Ash Rd CT13 28 D1
Ash Tree Cl CT7 17 E3
Ash Walk CT11 24 D5
Ashbee Gdns CT6 13 E1
Ashburn Gdns CT6 13 E2
Ashburnham Rd CT11 24 C4
Ashdown Cl CT6 13 E5
Ashdown Field CT4 39 A2
Ashenden Cl CT1 34 C5
Ashendene Gro CT2 33 E1
Ashford Rd, Canterbury CT1 34 A5
Ashford Rd, Chartham CT4 39 A1
Ashley Cl CT12 24 C1
Ashley Dr CT5 8 B5
Ashton Ct CT10 23 E3
Ashton Mws CT10 5 C4
Ashtrees CT6 12 D3
Ashurst Av CT5 8 D5
Ashurst Gdns CT9 21 E2
Aspen Rd, Canterbury CT4 39 C3
Aspen Rd, Herne Bay CT6 14 B2
Aspinall Cl CT4 37 C2
Astor Rd CT10 21 E6
Athelstan Rd, Canterbury CT1 34 C5
Athelstan Rd, Margate CT9 3 F2
Athena Ct CT9 20 A2
Athol Rd CT5 9 G2
Auckland Av CT12 24 B1
Audley Av CT9 18 C4
Augusta Pl CT11 4 E1
Augusta Rd CT11 4 E1
Augustine Rd CT12 15 A5
Aunt Betsys Hill CT4 37 B4
Aurelie Way CT5 9 G5
Austin Av CT6 11 E2
Austins La*, New St CT13 29 F2
Avebury Av CT11 25 G2
Avenue Gdns CT9 20 B3
Avenue Rd, Herne Bay CT6 12 A2
Avenue Rd, Ramsgate CT11 25 G3
Avon Cl CT1 36 A2
Avondale Cl CT5 9 H4
Aynsley Ct CT13 29 F1
Ayrshire Ct CT2 31 F6
Ayton Rd CT11 4 A2

Babs Oak Hill CT2 33 E1
Back La CT1 6 A4
Baddlesmere Rd CT5 9 H1
Badgers Cl CT2 30 A1
Bairds Hill CT10 23 F2
Bairdsley Cl CT10 5 A1
Bakers Cl CT2 34 C3
Bakers Ct CT11 4 D1
Bakers La CT4 39 B3
Balcomb Cres CT9 20 B6
Baliol Rd CT5 9 G2
Balliemoor Ct CT11 25 F1
Balliemoor Ct*, Argyll Dr CT11 25 F1
Balliol Rd CT10 21 E6
Balmoral Pl CT11 4 E1
Balmoral Rd CT9 18 C5
Bank St CT6 12 C1
Barbers Almshouses CT11 4 B2
Barclay Ct CT8 18 C4
Barley Cl CT6 13 F5
Barn Cl CT5 7 A3
Barn Cotts CT2 31 E1
Barn Cres CT9 18 C4
Barnes Av CT9 18 C4
Barnes Ct CT1 34 D4
Barnes Way CT6 13 H2
Barnesende Ct CT13 29 F2
Barnfield CT6 11 H4
Barrington Cres CT7 17 F3
Barrows Cl CT7 17 E4
Bartlett Dr CT5 9 H3
Barton Bsns Pk CT1 36 B4
Barton Mill Ct CT2 6 B1
Barton Mill Rd CT1 31 H6
Barton Rd CT1 36 A4
Bastien Mews CT1 36 A4
Bath Pl CT9 3 F2
Bath Rd CT9 3 E2
Bathurst Cl CT12 24 C1
Bawden Cl CT2 31 G4
Bay Ct CT5 9 H1
Bay View Heights CT7 16 B2
Bay View Rd CT10 23 F6
Bay Vw CT6 12 B1
Bayside Heights CT10 21 G4
Bayview Rd CT5 9 E5
Beach Av CT7 16 D3
Beach Ct, Westgate-on-Sea CT8 18 A3
Beach Ct, Broadstairs CT10 5 C3
Beach Houses CT9 3 A3
Beach Rd CT8 18 B3
Beach Rise CT9 18 B3
Beach St CT6 12 B1
Beach Walk CT5 9 F1
Beacon Av CT6 13 E1
Beacon Heights CT5 9 G1
Beacon Hill CT6 12 D1
Beacon La CT13 28 A4
Beacon Rd, Broadstairs CT10 23 E2
Beacon Rd, Herne Bay CT6 12 D2
Beacon Walk CT6 12 D1
Beaconsfield Gdns CT10 23 F3
Beaconsfield Rd CT2 31 F6
Beaconsfields CT5 8 A6
Beadle Cl CT6 12 D3
Beamont Cl CT12 26 A2
Beatrice Rd CT9 19 F4
Beaufort Av CT12 24 C2
Beaumanor CT6 12 C4
Beaumont St CT6 11 G2
Becket Av CT2 34 D1
Becket Cl, Canterbury CT3 27 C2
Becket Cl, Whitstable CT5 10 A5
Becket Mews CT2 6 A2
Bedford Ct CT10 5 D1
Bedford Dr CT6 12 D4
Bedford Sq CT12 24 C1
Bedford Way CT7 14 C6
Bedlam Court La CT12 15 C6
Beech Av CT4 39 D3
Beech Ct CT1 6 D6
Beech Dr CT10 22 C4
Beech Gro CT12 26 B6
Beech Hill CT4 37 C5
Beechcroft CT5 10 C5
Beechcroft Gdns CT11 25 G2
Beecroft Cl CT2 31 G3
Beer Cart La CT1 6 B4
Bekesbourne Hill CT4 37 C1
Bekesbourne La, Canterbury CT3 36 C2
Bekesbourne La, Littlebourne CT3 38 A3
Bekesbourne Rd CT4 37 A3
Belgrave Cl CT11 25 E3
Belgrave Rd CT9 3 C3
Bell Davies Dr CT12 26 A2
Bell La*, The Quay CT13 29 F2
Belle Vue Cotts CT6 13 F4
Belle Vue Rd CT6 12 D2
Bellevue Av CT11 4 E1
Bellevue Rd, Ramsgate CT11 4 E1
Bellevue Rd, Whitstable CT5 9 G4
Bellflower Mews CT1 35 H4
Belmont Ct CT11 25 E3
Belmont Ho CT11 24 D5
Belmont Rd, Broadstairs CT10 5 B3
Belmont Rd, Ramsgate CT11 25 E3
Belmont Rd, Westgate-on-Sea CT8 18 B5
Belmont Rd, Whitstable CT5 9 E3
Belmont St CT11 4 D1
Belmont Ter CT13 27 B5
Belmont Yd CT5 9 F3
Beltinge Rd CT6 12 C2
Belton Cl CT5 9 F4
Belvedere Rd CT10 5 C4
Benacre Rd CT5 9 E6
Bengal Rd CT12 24 B1
Benjamin Villas CT7 14 B6
Bennells Av CT5 10 A4
Benson Ho CT1 6 A5
Benstede Cl CT6 12 C6
Bentley Av CT6 11 F2
Beresford Gap CT7 16 D2
Beresford Gdns CT9 20 B2
Beresford Rd, Ramsgate CT11 4 B2
Beresford Rd, Whitstable CT5 9 F3
Berkeley Rd CT7 16 D2
Best La CT1 6 B3
Beverley Ho CT2 31 F6
Beverley Rd CT2 31 E6
Beverley Way CT12 24 D2
Beverly Cl CT7 17 F3
Bexley St CT5 9 E2
Bhutan Rd CT6 13 F3
Bicknor Cl CT2 31 H4
Biddenden Cl CT9 20 B4
Biddenden Cl*, Tenterden Wy CT9 20 B4
Bierce Ct CT7 16 D3
Bifrons Gdns CT4 37 C3
Bifrons Hill CT4 37 B2
Bifrons Rd CT4 37 C2
Bigglestons Link CT1 6 D4
Bilton Sq CT9 3 C2
Bingley Ct CT1 6 A5
Binnie Cl CT10 23 F6
Birch Cl CT10 22 C5
Birch Hill Ct CT7 17 F4
Birch Lodge CT6 12 C2
Birch Rd, Whitstable CT5 9 H4
Birch Rd, Canterbury CT1 35 E5
Birchwood Walk CT2 31 E6
Birds Av CT9 18 C5
Birkdale Cl CT5 10 C6
Birkdale Gdns CT6 12 A5
Birons Path CT4 37 B5
Bishopden Ct CT2 30 C4
Bishops Av CT10 23 G2
Bishops Courtyard CT1 6 D4
Bishops Way CT2 34 D1
Bishopstone Dr CT6 13 H1
Bishopstone La CT6 13 H2
Black Griffin La CT1 6 A3
Black La CT13 28 D3
Blackberry Way CT5 10 A6
Blackburn Rd CT6 11 F3
Blackfriars St CT1 6 C2
Blackthorn Rd CT3 38 A5
Blean Common CT2 30 A1
Blean Hill CT2 30 A2
Blean View Rd CT6 11 G4
Blenheim Av CT1 36 B1
Blenheim Cl, Broadstairs CT10 22 D5
Blenheim Cl, Herne Bay CT6 12 C6
Bloomsbury Rd CT11 24 D4
Blossom Ct CT2 32 D3
Blueberry Cl CT10 23 F6
Bluefield Mews CT5 9 E6
Bobbin Lodge Hill CT4 39 A3
Bognor Dr CT6 12 A3
Bogshole La, Herne Bay CT6 13 F4
Bogshole La, Whitstable CT5 7 E2
Boleyn Av CT9 18 B4
Bolton St CT11 25 E3
Bolts Hill CT4 39 A2
Booth Pl CT9 3 E2
Borrowdale Av CT11 24 B4
Borstal Av CT5 9 E6
Borstal Hill CT5 9 E4
Bossenden Ct CT2 30 C4
Botany Rd CT10 21 E4
Botelar Cotts CT13 27 A6
Boughton Av CT10 25 H1
Boundary Chase CT3 10 A6
Boundary Ct CT1 35 H4
Boundary Rd CT11 25 E3
Bourne Lodge Cl CT2 30 A1
Bourne Park Rd CT4 37 B6
Bourne Vw CT4 37 A5
Bournemouth Dr CT6 11 H1
Bowen Ct CT11 4 A1
Bowes Av CT9 18 B4
Bowes La CT6 12 C4
Bowland Cl CT6 13 E5
Bowling St CT13 29 E1
Bowyer Rd CT5 8 A5
Boystown Pl CT13 27 C5
Brabourne Cl CT2 31 G3
Bracken Ct CT10 23 E3
Bradley Rd CT12 24 D2
Bradstow Way CT10 5 A1
Braggs La CT6 14 A3
Bramblefields Cl CT6 13 E5
Bramley Av CT1 34 C4
Bramley Gdns CT6 13 F4
Bramshaw Rd CT2 31 E6
Brandon Rd CT12 24 B1
Brandon Way CT7 17 F4
Brassey Av CT10 5 A6
Brecon Sq CT12 24 B1
Brewers Pl CT13 27 D3
Brewery La CT4 37 B5
Briars Walk CT10 23 F5
Briary Cl CT9 18 B4
Brice Av CT4 39 B3
Brices Alley CT5 9 E2
Bridewell Pk CT5 9 H3
Bridge By-Pass CT4 37 A3
Bridge Cl CT13 29 F1
Bridge Down CT4 37 C6
Bridge Hill CT4 37 B5
Bridge Rd CT9 18 C4
Bridgefield Ct CT5 10 A3
Bridgefield Rd CT5 10 A3
Bridgeford Way CT4 37 B5
Bridger Ct CT7 17 E2
Bridges Cl CT7 14 B5
Bridle Way CT6 12 A4
Bridleway Gdns CT10 22 D5
Brightlingsea Rd CT13 29 E2
Brights Pl CT11 25 F3
Brindle Gro CT11 25 G2
Brisbane Dr CT12 24 B1
Bristol Pl CT11 4 C1
Bristol Rd CT1 35 F3
Britannia Av CT5 8 C5
Broad Oak Rd CT2 31 G6
Broad St, Canterbury CT1 6 D2
Broad St, Margate CT9 3 D2
Broad St, Ramsgate CT11 4
Broadlands CT2 32
Broadlands Ind Est CT2 30
Broadley Av CT7 16
Broadley Rd CT9 20
Broadstairs Rd CT10 23
Broadstairs Retail Pk CT10 22
Brockenhurst Cl CT2 31
Brockenhurst Rd CT11 25
Brockley Rd CT9 3
Brockmans Cl CT12 15
Bromstone Mews CT10 23
Bromstone Rd CT10 23
Brook Cl CT6 11
Brook Rd CT5 10
Brook St CT13 27
Brooke Av CT9 18
Brooklands Cl CT2 32
Brooksend Cotts CT7 16
Broomfield Cres CT9 21
Broomfield Rd CT6 13
Brotherhood Cl*, Giles La CT2 30
Brotherwood Cl CT2 30
Brownings Yd CT5 9
Brundell Ter CT4 39
Brunswick Ct CT11 4
Brunswick Rd CT7 17
Brunswick Sq CT6 12
Brunswick St CT11 4
Brymore Cl CT1 31
Brymore Rd CT1 31
Buckhurst Dr CT9 21
Buckingham Rd, Broadsta CT10 5
Buckingham Rd, Margate CT9 19
Buckingham Rd, Whitstabl CT5 10
Buenos Ayres CT9 3
Builders Sq CT3 38
Bullers Av CT6 12
Bullockstone Rd CT6 12
Burch Av CT13 29
Burfords Alley CT3 27
Burgate CT1 6
Burgate La CT1 6
Burgess Cl CT12 15
Burlington Dr CT6 13
Burlington Gdns CT9 18
Burma Cres CT1 36
Burnan Rd CT5 10
Bursill Cres CT12 24
Burton Flds CT6 13
Bush Av CT12 24
Busheyfields Rd CT6 14
Bushy Hill Rd CT2 33
Butchery La CT1 6
Buxton Rd CT12 22
Byron Av CT9 3
Byron Cl CT1 36

Cadnam Cl CT2 31
Caernarvon Gdns CT10 5
Calais Hill CT2 31
Calcraft Mews CT1 31
Caledon Ter CT1 6
Callis Court Rd CT10 23
Calverden Rd CT12 24
Cambourne Av CT8 17
Cambrai Ct CT1 36
Cambrian Cotts CT11 4
Cambridge Cl CT7 17
Cambridge Rd CT1 35
Cambridge Way CT1 35
Camden Rd, Broadstairs CT10 20
Camden Rd, Ramsgate CT11 4
Camden Sq CT11 4
Camelia Cl CT9 18
Campbell Cl CT6 13
Campfield CT6 12
Cannon Rd CT11 4
Cannonbury Rd CT11 4

nterbury By-Pass T1,2 34 A2
nterbury Cl CT10 22 D3
nterbury Hill CT2 31 E2
nterbury Ind Pk T3 38 C5
nterbury La CT1 6 C4
nterbury Rd, Birchington T7 16 B6
nterbury Rd, Herne T6 14 B3
nterbury Rd, Herne Bay T6 12 C4,5
nterbury Rd, Margate T9 18 A5
nterbury Rd, : Nicholas at Wade T7 14 C6
nterbury Rd, /estgate-on-Sea T8 17 G3
nterbury Rd, Whitstable T5 9 E4
nterbury Rd East T11 24 A4
nterbury Rd West T12 26 A4
nterbury Retail Pk T1 32 B4
nterbury Road rchington CT7 16 C6
nterbury Road largate CT8,9 18 B4
nterbury Road, Westgate T8 17 G3
nute Rd CT7 16 B3
pel Cl CT10 21 F4
rey Ho CT1 6 A5
rlton Av, Broadstairs T10 5 B2
rlton Av, Ramsgate T11 4 B2
rlton Hill CT6 11 G1
rlton Mansions T9 19 H1
rlton Rd CT5 7 D4
rlton Rd East CT8 17 H2
rlton Rd West CT8 17 G2
rlton Rise CT8 17 G2
rmel Cl CT4 39 A2
rmel Ct*, Gainsboro Rd T7 16 D2
rnoustie Cl CT5 10 C6
roline Cl CT5 8 C6
roline Cres CT10 23 E2
roline Sq CT9 3 F2
rriage Mews CT2 6 B1
rroways Pl CT9 3 E3
rtwright Cl CT3 27 B2
astle Av CT10 23 G2
astle Rd CT5 9 G1
astle Row CT1 6 B5
astle St CT1 6 A5
astle View CT10 21 G4
athedral Vw CT2 31 G6
atherine Way CT10 23 F2
attle Mkt CT13 29 E2
avendish Ct CT6 12 C2
avendish Pl CT11 4 C2
avendish Rd CT6 12 C2
avendish St CT11 4 C1
axton Rd CT9 18 D5
ecil Ct CT6 12 D2
ecil Pk CT6 12 C2
ecil Sq CT9 3 D3
ecil St CT9 3 D3
ecilia Gro CT10 23 E2
ecilia Rd CT11 25 F2
edar Cl, Broadstairs CT10 21 E6
edar Cl, Margate CT9 20 B4
edar Cl, Birchington CT7 17 E3
edar Lodge CT6 12 C2
edar Rd CT2 32 D2
edarview CT2 34 C1
edric Rd CT8 17 H2
entenary Gdns CT13 27 B6
entral Av CT6 11 H1
entral Par CT6 12 A2
entral Rd CT11 25 E2
hafy Cres CT2 32 D3
halet Gate CT11 4 A1
halfont Dr CT6 13 F5
halk Hill CT12 24 A4
hallock Ct CT9 21 E3
hamberlain Dr CT6 11 G1

Chancel Ct CT2 34 D1
Chanctonbury Chase CT5 8 B6
Chandos Rd CT10 5 C4
Chandos Sq CT10 5 C4
Channel Rd CT9 22 A2
Chantry Ct CT1 6 C2
Chapel Cotts CT6 13 F4
Chapel Hill CT9 19 H6
Chapel Hill Cl CT9 19 H6
Chapel La, Blean CT2 30 A1
Chapel La, Broad Oak CT2 32 B1
Chapel La, Sturry CT2 32 C3
Chapel Pl, Birchington CT7 17 E4
Chapel Pl, Ramsgate CT11 4 B2
Chapel Place La CT11 4 B1
Chapel Rd CT11 24 D3
Chapel Row CT6 14 D1
Chapel St CT6 12 C1
Chaplains Way CT4 39 D3
Chapman Fields CT12 26 C6
Charing Cl CT12 24 D2
Charing Cres CT8 17 H3
Charles Rd CT11 25 F2
Charles St CT6 12 C1
Charlestown Ct CT10 5 C5
Charlesworth Dr CT7 17 E3
Charlotte Ct CT11 4 D2
Charlotte Mews*, Gordon Rd CT1 6 A6
Charlotte Mws CT1 6 A6
Charlotte Pl CT9 3 D4
Charlotte Sq CT9 3 D4
Charlotte St CT10 5 C4
Charlton Cl CT12 22 B6
Charnwood CT5 10 C5
Charollais Cl CT2 31 G5
Chartham Ter CT11 4 B4
Chartwell Av CT6 13 F3
Chatham Pl CT11 25 E3
Chatham St CT11 25 E3
Chatsworth Mews CT11 4 A2
Chaucer Av CT5 10 A4
Chaucer Cl CT1 36 A3
Chaucer Hospital CT1 35 G6
Chaucer Rd, Broadstairs CT10 5 A5
Chaucer Rd, Canterbury CT1 35 H1
Chaucer Wood Ct CT1 35 H1
Cheesmans Cl CT12 15 C6
Chelsea Rd CT1 32 A4
Chequer La CT3 27 B2
Cheriton Av CT12 24 C2
Cherry Av CT2 30 D6
Cherry Ct CT10 21 E6
Cherry Dr CT2 30 D6
Cherry Garden La CT3 27 D2
Cherry Garden Rd CT2 30 D6
Cherry Gdns, Broadstairs CT10 22 C5
Cherry Gdns, Herne Bay CT6 12 B3
Cherry Orchard, Canterbury CT3 38 B1
Cherry Orchard, Whitstable CT5 10 B6
Cherry Orchard Mws CT3 38 B1
Cherry Tree Ct CT5 9 H1
Cherry Tree Gdns CT12 22 B5
Cherville La CT3 38 D2
Chester Rd CT8 18 B4
Chestfield Rd CT5 10 B5
Chestnut Av CT2 30 A1
Chestnut Dr, Broadstairs CT10 22 D4
Chestnut Dr, Canterbury CT2 33 E1
Chestnut Dr, Deal CT14 29 F6
Chestnut Dr, Herne Bay CT6 11 H4
Cheviot Ct CT10 5 D1
Chichester Rd CT12 24 C1
Chichester Walk CT12 24 C1
Childgate Rd CT5 7 A4

Chilham Av CT8 17 H3
Chilton Fld CT3 27 B2
Chilton Gdns CT3 27 B2
Chilton La CT11 24 B5
Chilton Pl CT3 27 B2
Chilton Sq CT3 27 B2
Chineham Way CT1 35 F4
Chislet Cl CT3 38 D5
Chislet Ct CT6 12 A2
Chislet Park Cotts CT3 38 C2
Christopher Villas CT7 14 B6
Chrysler Av CT6 11 F2
Church Av CT11 4 A3
Church Cotts CT7 14 C6
Church Court Gro CT10 22 D2
Church Farm Way CT13 28 A4
Church Hill, Canterbury CT2 34 C1
Church Hill, Ramsgate CT11 4 C1
Church La, Canterbury CT1 6 A5
Church La, Canterbury CT1 6 C2
Church La, Chartham CT4 39 C1
Church La, Seasalter CT5 8 B6
Church La, Sturry CT2 32 C3
Church La, Westbere CT2 33 F1
Church Rd, Broadstairs CT10 5 C3
Church Rd, Canterbury CT3 38 B2
Church Rd, Margate CT9 3 E4
Church Rd, Ramsgate CT11 4 D1
Church Sq CT10 5 D3
Church St, Broadstairs CT10 23 E3
Church St, Eastry CT13 27 C6
Church St, Margate CT9 3 E4
Church St, Ramsgate CT12 15 B6
Church St, St Dunstans CT2 35 E1
Church St, St Pauls CT1 6 D4
Church St, Whitstable CT5 9 G3
Church St, Woodnesborough CT13 28 A5
Church St*, St Clements CT13 29 F2
Church Street St Marys CT13 29 E1
Church Vw, Herne Bay CT6 13 F3
Church Vw, Sandwich CT13 29 G6
Church Way CT5 10 C3
Church Wood Cl CT2 30 B6
Churchfield Pl CT9 3 D3
Churchfields, Broadstairs CT10 21 E6
Churchfields, Margate CT9 3 D4
Churchill Av CT6 13 F2
Churchill Cl CT4 37 A5
Churchill Ct, Ramsgate CT11 25 E3
Churchill Ct, Canterbury CT2 31 F5
Churchill Rd CT1 35 H4
Churchwood Dr CT5 10 C5
Cinder Ho CT10 5 A3
Cinder Path CT10 5 A3
Citroen Cl CT6 11 F2
City Bsns Pk CT1 32 A5
City Vw CT2 34 D2
City Wall Av CT1 6 A4
Claire Ct, Broadstairs CT10 5 C2
Claire Ct, Birchington CT7 16 D3
Clapham Hill CT5 7 D1
Clare Dr CT6 11 G4
Clare Rd CT5 9 F1

Claremont Gdns CT11 24 D3
Claremont Pl CT1 6 A6
Claremont St CT6 11 H2
Claremont Ter CT13 28 C3
Claremont Way CT3 38 D4
Clarence Av CT9 20 C3
Clarence Rd, Herne Bay CT6 12 A2
Clarence Rd, Ramsgate CT11 24 C5
Clarence St CT6 12 B2
Clarendon Gdns CT11 4 C2
Clarendon Mews CT10 5 A3
Clarendon Rd, Broadstairs CT10 5 A3
Clarendon Rd, Margate CT9 19 H2
Clarendon St CT6 11 G2
Cleaver La CT11 4 D1
Clement Cl CT1 31 H6
Clementine Cl CT6 13 F2
Clements Rd CT12 22 C6
Cleve Ct CT12 15 B2
Cliff Av CT6 13 F1
Cliff Dr CT6 11 H2
Cliff Fld CT8 17 G2
Cliff Prom CT10 21 H6
Cliff Rd, Birchington CT7 16 C2
Cliff Rd, Broadstairs CT10 23 H1
Cliff Rd, Whitstable CT5 9 G1
Cliff Sea Gro CT6 11 H2
Cliff St CT11 4 C2
Cliff Ter CT9 3 F1
Cliff View Rd CT12 26 B5
Cliffe Av CT9 18 D3
Clifford Rd CT5 9 G4
Cliffsend Gro CT12 26 C6
Cliffsend Rd CT12 26 C6
Cliffside Dr CT10 25 H1
Clifftown Gdns CT6 11 G2
Clift Mews CT9 19 H1
Clifton Gdns, Canterbury CT2 30 D6
Clifton Gdns, Margate CT9 3 F2
Clifton Lawn CT11 4 B4
Clifton Pl CT9 3 F2
Clifton Rd, Margate CT9 3 F2
Clifton Rd, Ramsgate CT11 24 C3
Clifton Rd, Whitstable CT5 9 E3
Clifton St CT9 3 E2
Cliftonville Av, Margate CT9 20 A3
Cliftonville Av, Ramsgate CT12 24 C2
Cliftonville Ct CT11 19 H1
Clive Rd, Margate CT9 22 A3
Clive Rd, Ramsgate CT12 26 B5
Cliveden Pl CT10 23 E3
Cloveley Lodge*, Moss End Mws CT12 23 E6
Clovelly Rd CT5 9 E5
Clover Rise CT5 10 A4
Clowes Ct CT2 30 C4
Clyde La CT1 35 F3
Clyde St CT1 35 G1
Coach House Mws CT9 20 A2
Coastguard Alley CT5 8 D2
Coastguard Cotts CT11 24 B5
Cobblers Bridge Rd CT6 12 A3
Cobbs Pl CT9 3 D2
Cobden Pl CT1 6 C2
Cobham Cl CT1 36 A4
Cockering Rd, Canterbury CT1 34 A6
Cockering Rd, Chartham CT4 39 C3
Codrington Rd CT11 4 A2
Cogans Ter CT1 35 E3
Coggan Ho CT1 6 A5
Colburn Rd CT10 25 H1
Cold Harbour CT1 6 D1
Coleman Cres CT12 24 D1

Colemans Stairs CT7 17 E2
Colemans Stairs Rd CT7 17 E2
Colemans Yd CT11 4 C2
Colette Cl CT10 21 F3
Colette Ho CT11 4 C1
Colewood Rd CT5 10 D3
Collar Makers Grn CT13 27 D3
Collard Cl CT6 12 D3
Collard Ho CT1 36 A2
College Ct CT1 35 H1
College Farm Cotts CT7 16 C6
College Gdns CT8 18 A5
College Rd, Canterbury CT1 35 H1
College Rd, Margate CT9 19 F5
College Rd, Ramsgate CT11 25 E2
College Sq CT9 3 D2
College Walk CT9 3 D2
Collingwood Cl, Broadstairs CT10 23 E4
Collingwood Cl, Westgate-on-Sea CT8 17 G3
Collingwood Rd CT5 9 E3
Collins Rd CT6 11 H4
Colombo Sq CT12 24 B1
Columbia Av CT5 8 C5
Columbine Cl CT5 8 D6
Columbus Av CT12 15 C2
Conference Walk CT1 36 A2
Conference Walk*, Russett Rd CT1 36 A2
Conifer Ct CT8 18 B4
Coniston Av CT11 24 B4
Connaught Gdns CT9 19 G4
Connaught Rd CT9 19 G4
Conrad Av CT1 32 A5
Constable Rd CT7 16 D2
Consul Cl CT6 11 F2
Convent Rd CT10 21 E5
Convent Walk CT11 24 C5
Conway Cl CT7 16 C3
Conyngham Cl CT12 24 C1
Conyngham La CT4 37 B4
Conyngham Rd, Herne Bay CT6 13 F1
Conyngham Rd, Ramsgate CT12 15 B6
Cooks Lea CT13 27 B5
Coombe La CT3 27 D3
Coombe Walk CT5 7 A4
Coopers Hill*, Charles St CT6 12 C1
Coopers La CT1 35 E3
Cop Street Rd CT3 27 C1
Copinger Cl CT2 31 G4
Copperas Ct CT5 9 H1
Copperfield Ct, Broadstairs CT10 5 D3
Copperfield Ct, CanterburyCT1 6 D5
Coppergate CT2 31 F6
Copperhurst Walk CT9 21 E3
Coppock Cl CT12 24 C1
Copt Cl CT2 32 D1
Cordingham Cl CT5 8 C6
Cormorant Way CT6 13 H2
Cornelis Dr CT12 15 B6
Cornford Rd CT7 17 E4
Cornhill CT11 4 C3
Cornwall Av CT11 25 G2
Cornwall Gdns, Canterbury CT1 36 A3
Cornwall Gdns, Margate CT9 20 B3
Cornwall Rd CT6 11 G4
Cornwallis Av CT6 13 E3
Cornwallis Circle CT5 9 E3
Cornwallis Gdns CT10 23 G2
Coronation Cl CT10 21 E6
Coronation Cres CT9 18 C4
Coronation Rd CT11 4 A2
Corsican Walk*, Cornwallis Wk CT6 13 F3
Corylus Dr CT5 8 C5
Cossington Rd CT1 6 D5
Cottage Rd CT11 4 D2

Cottage Row CT13 29 E1
Cottington La CT12 26 A6
Cottington Rd CT12 26 A6
Cotton Rd CT1 34 D3
Coulter Rd CT6 11 G4
Countess Mountbatten Ct CT8 18 A5
Court Cotts CT7 14 B5
Court Hill CT3 38 A1
Court Mdws CT3 38 A2
Court Rd CT7 14 A5
Courtlands CT6 12 D3
Courtlands Cl CT12 26 C6
Courtlands Way CT8 18 A3
Coventon La CT13 29 F5
Coventry Gdns CT6 13 G1
Cow La CT1 34 D3
Cowdrey Pl CT1 35 H4
Cowley Rise CT9 20 B6
Cowper Cl CT5 10 C3
Cowper Rd CT9 3 E4
Coxes Av CT12 22 B5
Coxes La CT12 22 B5
Craddock Dr CT1 35 H1
Craddock Rd CT1 35 H1
Crampton Ct CT10 5 A3
Cranbourne Cl CT11 25 G2
Cranbourne Walk CT2 31 E5
Cranbrook Cl CT9 21 E4
Cranleigh Gdns CT5 9 F4
Cranmer Cl CT4 37 C2
Cranmer Ho CT2 35 E1
Cravel Walk CT1 6 C4
Craven Cl CT9 18 D5
Crawford Gdns CT9 20 A3
Crawford Rd CT10 23 F3
Creine Mill Lane North CT1 6 A4
Creine Mill Lane South CT1 6 A4
Cremer Cl CT4 39 B2
Crescent Ho CT9 3 F2
Crescent Rd, Birchington CT7 17 E3
Crescent Rd, Broadstairs CT10 21 G5
Crescent Rd, Margate CT9 3 A3
Crescent Rd, Ramsgate CT11 4 A1
Cresta Cl CT6 11 E2
Crinan Ct CT11 25 G1
Crispe Ho CT7 16 D3
Crispe Park Cl CT7 17 E3
Crispe Rd CT7 16 C6
Crofton Rd CT8 18 A5
Crofts Pl CT10 5 C3
Cromwell Rd, Canterbury CT1 35 G4
Cromwell Rd, Whitstable CT5 9 E3
Cross Keys CT4 39 A2
Cross Rd CT7 17 E3
Cross St, Canterbury CT2 35 E1
Cross St, Herne Bay CT6 12 A3
Crossley Av CT6 11 E2
Crossways CT2 31 F4
Crossways Av CT9 22 A3
Crow Hill CT10 5 B1
Crow Hill Rd CT9 18 C5
Crown Gdns CT2 35 E1
Crown Hill Rd CT6 11 G2
Crundale Way CT9 21 E4
Crystal Bsns Centre CT13 29 G1
Cudham Gdns CT9 20 D3
Culpepper CT2 31 G4
Cumberland Av, Broadstairs CT10 5 B1
Cumberland Av, Canterbury CT1 36 B3
Cumberland Rd, Margate CT9 20 A3
Cumberland Rd, Ramsgate CT11 4 A2
Cundishall Cl CT5 8 D4
Cunningham Cres CT7 16 C3
Curlew Cl CT6 13 E4
Curlinge Ct CT11 24 B5
Curtis Wood Park Rd CT6 14 C2
Curtis Wood Rd CT6 14 C2
Curzon Ho CT11 4 B2
Cushman Rd CT1 35 E3
Cuthbert Rd CT8 17 H2
Cypress Cl CT5 8 D5

Daigor La CT12 26 D3
Daimler Av CT6 11 F2
Dalby Rd CT9 3 F2
Dalby Sq CT9 3 F2
Dallinger Rd CT7 16 D2
Dalmaney Cl CT10 5 C2
Dalmeny Av CT9 20 C4
Dalton Ct CT11 4 D1
Damerham Cl CT2 31 E5
Dane Court Gdns CT10 22 D2
Dane Court Rd CT10 22 C1
Dane Cres CT11 25 F2
Dane End Rd CT8 17 H2
Dane Gdns CT9 20 B6
Dane Hill CT9 3 E2
Dane Hill Gro CT9 3 E2
Dane Hill Row CT9 3 E2
Dane John Cotts CT1 6 B6
Dane John Ct CT1 6 B5
Dane John Mews CT1 6 B5
Dane Mt CT9 20 B6
Dane Park Rd, Margate CT9 3 F3
Dane Park Rd, Ramsgate CT11 25 F2
Dane Rd, Birchington CT7 16 A3
Dane Rd, Margate CT9 3 E2
Dane Rd, Ramsgate CT11 25 F3
Dane Valley Rd CT9 20 A5
Danehurst CT8 17 H1
Danepark CT9 3 E3
Danesmead Ter CT9 3 F3
Daniels Ct CT5 8 D3
Darenth Cl CT6 12 D4
Dargate Rd CT5 7 A4
Darnley Cl CT10 23 F5
Darrell Cl CT6 11 H3
Darren Gdns CT10 25 G1
Darwin Ct CT9 20 A2
Darwin Rd, Birchington CT7 16 D3
Darwin Rd, Canterbury CT2 31 E3
Daryngton Av CT7 16 A3
David Av CT9 20 C3
Davids Cl CT10 5 C5
Davidson Rd CT2 34 D1
Daytona Way CT6 11 E2
De L'Angle Row CT4 39 C1
Deal Rd CT13 29 E5
Dean Cft CT6 13 E5
Dean Ct CT1 6 D2
Deane Cl CT5 9 F5
Deanery Cotts CT4 39 B2
Deanery Farm Oast CT4 39 B2
Deansway Av CT2 32 C1
Deborah Cl CT5 9 G5
Deers Pk CT10 25 H1
Delacourt Cl CT12 26 B6
Delaware Cl CT2 32 D2
Delf St CT13 29 E1
Delfside CT13 29 F3
Delmar Cl CT5 10 C3
Denbigh Rd CT12 24 B2
Dence Cl CT6 12 D2
Dence Pk CT6 12 D2
Dene Walk CT9 19 G5
Denmark Rd CT11 25 F3
Denne Cl CT2 32 D1
Denstead Ct CT2 30 C4
Dent-de-Lion Ct CT9 18 B5
Dent-de-Lion Rd, Margate CT9 18 C5
Dent-de-Lion Rd, Westgate-on-Sea CT8 17 H2
Denton Way CT9 20 B4
Dering Cl CT4 37 B4
Dering Rd, Canterbury CT4 37 B4
Dering Rd, Herne Bay CT6 12 B2
Derwent Av CT11 24 B4
D'Este Rd CT11 4 F1
Detling Av CT10 25 G1
Devon Ct CT12 24 C1
Devon Ct*, Stirling Way CT12 24 C1
Devon Gdns CT7 16 D4
Devon Rd CT1 36 A2
Devonshire Gdns CT9 20 B3
Devonshire Ter CT10 5 C3
Dextor Cl CT2 31 F6
Diamond Ho CT5 9 F2
Diamond Rd CT5 9 F2
Dickens Av CT1 32 A6
Dickens Ct CT9 20 A2
Dickens Lodge CT10 22 D3
Dickens Rd CT10 5 C2
Dickens Walk CT10 5 C3
Discovery Walk CT1 36 A3
Discovery Walk*, Russett Rd CT1 36 A2
Doggerel Acre CT5 9 G5
Dolphin Cl CT10 21 F3
Dolphin Ct CT6 12 B1
Dolphin St CT6 12 B1
Dominic Ct CT10 23 E3
Domneva Rd, Ramsgate CT12 15 B5
Domneva Rd, Westgate-on-Sea CT8 17 H2
Donegal Rd CT1 36 A2
Donnahay Rd CT12 22 C5
Dorcas Gdns CT10 23 G2
Doric Ct CT11 24 D5
Dorothy Ct CT7 17 E4
Dorothy Dr CT12 22 C6
Dorset Cl CT5 8 C5
Dorset Ct CT12 24 C1
Dorset Gdns CT7 16 D4
Dorset Rd CT1 36 B3
Douglas Av CT5 9 F3
Douglas Cl CT10 23 E3
Douglas Rd CT6 12 C3
Douro Cl CT1 36 B1
Dove Cl, Herne Bay CT6 14 B2
Dove Cl, Whitstable CT5 8 D5
Dove Ct CT11 4 D1
Dovedale Ct CT7 17 F4
Dover Rd CT13 28 D5
Dover St CT1 6 D4
Down Barton Rd CT7 14 A6
Downs Av CT5 9 F3
Downs Pk CT6 12 D2
Downs Rd, Canterbury CT2 31 F4
Downs Rd, Ramsgate CT11 24 B5
Downthorne Ho CT6 12 B2
Dragoon Ho CT1 6 D2
Drainless Rd CT13 28 A6
Drapers Almshouses CT9 19 H5
Drapers Av CT9 19 G4
Drapers Cl CT9 19 H5
Drill La CT3 38 C1
Drybeck Av CT11 24 A3
Dryden Cl CT1 36 A3
Drying Shed La CT1 6 A4
Duck La CT1 6 C2
Dudley Av CT8 17 G2
Duke St CT9 3 D2
Dumpton Gap Rd CT10 23 G6
Dumpton Ho CT10 23 F6
Dumpton La CT11 25 F2
Dumpton Park Dr CT11 25 G3
Duncan Cl CT5 9 E5
Duncan Dr CT7 16 C3
Duncan Rd, Ramsgate CT11 4 A2
Duncan Rd, Whitstable CT5 9 E4
Dundee Ho CT11 4 E2
Dundonald Rd, Broadstairs CT10 5 C4
Dundonald Rd, Ramsgate CT11 24 D4
Dunedin Rd CT12 24 B1
Dunoon Ct CT11 25 F1
Dunoon Ct*, Argyll Dr CT11 25 G1
Dunstan Av CT8 17 G4
Durban Cl CT12 24 B1
Durban Rd CT9 19 H4
Durham Cl CT1 35 F4
Durlock CT12 15 C6
Durlock Av CT11 24 C5
Durlock Rd CT3 27 A3
Durnford Cl CT2 31 E5
Durovernum Ct CT1 35 G3

Each End Cotts CT13 28 A1
Eagle Hill CT11 4 B1
Ealham Cl CT1 35 H5
Earlsmead Cres CT12 26 B6
East Cliff Par CT6 12 D1
East Cliff Prom CT10 23 H2
East Kent Retail Pk CT10 22 B3
East Northdown Cl CT9 21 E4
East St, Canterbury CT1 32 A5
East St, Herne Bay CT6 12 C1
East St, Sandwich CT13 28 A1
East View CT3 38 C5
Eastchurch Rd CT9 20 D3
Eastern Esp, Broadstairs CT10 23 H2
Eastern Esp, Margate CT9 20 A2
Eastfield Rd CT7 17 E3
Eastgate Cl CT6 12 D4
Eastry By-Pass CT13 27 D6
Eastry Mews CT13 27 B6
Eaton Hill CT9 3 C3
Eaton Rd CT9 19 F3
Eddie Willett Rd CT6 11 G3
Eddington Bsns Pk CT6 12 B4
Eddington La CT6 12 A3
Eddington Way CT6 12 B4
Eden Ct CT6 12 A2
Eden Rd CT5 8 B5
Edenfield CT7 17 F3
Edgar Cl CT5 10 C3
Edgar Rd, Canterbury CT1 35 H1
Edgar Rd, Margate CT9 19 H1
Edgar Rd, Ramsgate CT12 15 A5
Edge End Rd CT10 23 F4
Edinburgh Rd CT9 18 C5
Edinburgh Walk*, Edinburgh Rd CT9 18 C5
Edith Rd, Ramsgate CT11 24 D5
Edith Rd, Westgate-on-Sea CT8 18 A4
Edmanson Av CT9 18 B4
Edward Dr CT7 17 F3
Edward Rd CT1 35 G2
Effingham St CT11 4 C2
Egbert Rd, Birchington CT7 16 B3
Egbert Rd, Ramsgate CT11 15 B5
Egbert Rd, Westgate-on-Sea CT8 18 A4
Egerton Dr CT9 21 E3
Eider Cl CT6 12 A4
Eldon Gro CT11 4 A3
Eldon Pl CT10 5 D3
Elfrida Cl CT9 20 C5
Elgar Bretts Ct CT1 6 A6
Elgar Pl CT11 25 E3
Elham Cl*, Tenterden Way CT9 20 B4
Elham Ct CT9 20 B4
Elham Rd CT1 35 E4
Elham Way CT10 23 G6
Elisons Walk CT1 36 A2
Elizabeth Ct, Broadstairs CT10 23 H1
Elizabeth Ct, Canterbury CT1 35 H4
Elizabeth Kemp Ct CT12 24 D2
Elizabeth Rd CT11 4 E1
Elizabeth Way CT6 12 D3
Ellen Av CT11 25 F1
Ellen Ct CT3 38 B2
Ellenden Ct CT2 30 C4
Ellington Av CT9 18 C5
Ellington Cl CT8 17 H1
Ellington Pl CT11 24 D3
Ellington Rd CT11 4 A1
Elliot Cl CT1 32 A5
Elliot Ct CT6 13 E3
Elliot Ho CT6 13 E3
Ellis Rd CT5 10 A3
Ellis Way CT6 13 E4
Ellison Cl CT5 10 B5
Ellison Cl*, Russett Rd CT1 36
Elm Ct CT8 17
Elm Gro, Ramsgate CT12 26
Elm Gro, Westgate-on-Sea CT8 17
Elm Lodge CT6 12
Elm Wood Cl CT5 10
Elm Wood West CT5 10
Elmleigh Rd CT3 38
Elmley Way CT9 19
Elms Av CT11 4
Elms Ct CT1 35
Elmstone Gdns CT9 20
Elmstone Rd CT11 25
Elmwood Av CT10 21
Elmwood Cl CT10 21
Emelina Way CT5 8
Emmanuel Ct CT10 23
Emmerson Gdns CT5 10
Empire Ter CT9 19
Emptage Ct CT9 3
Enticott Cl CT5 9
Epping Cl CT6 12
Epple Bay Av CT7 17
Epple Bay Rd CT7 16
Epple Cottages St CT7 17
Epple Rd CT7 17
Ersham Rd CT1 35
Eskdale Av CT11 24
Esmonde Dr CT12 26
Esplanade CT8 17
Essex Av CT6 11
Essex Gdns CT7 16
Essex Rd, Canterbury CT1 36
Essex Rd, Westgate-on-Sea CT8 18
Essex St CT5 9
Estuary Way CT5 10
Ethel Rd CT10 5
Ethelbert Cres CT9 19
Ethelbert Gdns CT9 3
Ethelbert Rd, Birchington CT7 16
Ethelbert Rd, Canterbury CT1 35
Ethelbert Rd, Margate CT9 3
Ethelbert Rd, Ramsgate CT11 4
Ethelbert Sq CT8 18
Ethelbert Ter, Margate CT9 3
Ethelbert Ter, Westgate-on-Sea CT8 18
Ethelred Rd CT8 18
Evenhill Rd CT3 38
Eversleigh Rise CT5 9
Eynsford Cl CT9 21

Fair St CT10 23
Fairacre CT10 23
Fairacres Cl CT6 13
Fairfax Dr CT6 13
Fairfield Ct CT10 23
Fairfield Manor CT10 23
Fairfield Pk CT10 23
Fairfield Rd, Broadstairs CT10 23
Fairfield Rd, Minster CT12 15
Fairfield Rd, Ramsgate CT11 25
Fairlawn CT5 10
Fairlawn Rd CT12 22
Fairlight Av CT12 24
Fairoaks CT6 13
Fairview Cl CT9 3
Fairview Gdns CT2 33
Fairway Cres CT5 8
Falala Way CT1 35
Falcon Cl CT6 14
Farleigh Rd CT2 31
Farley Rd CT9 19
Farm House Cl CT5 9
Farrar Ct CT7 17
Farrar Rd CT7 17
Farthings Ct CT2 30
Faulkners La CT2 34
Faversham Rd CT5 8
Favourite Rd CT5 8
Felderland Cl CT14 29
Felderland La CT14 28

ɔulhet Way CT6 12 C2
Cl CT5 10 B5
Ct CT10 5 C2
dale Ct CT7 17 E4
down CT7 16 B2
lea Av CT6 12 A3
d Av CT1 32 A5
Vw CT5 8 C5
Way CT2 32 D3
ta Walk CT1 36 A2
a Walk*, Russett Rd
1 36 A2
Rd CT6 11 G3
Av CT9 20 B2
Tree Rd CT10 23 F1
er Rd CT4 37 B5
bury Rd CT11 25 F3
ree Cl CT11 24 D4
ree Hill CT13 28 A5
ank Gdns CT9 19 F5
anks CT5 9 H4
Av, Broadstairs
10 21 E3
Av, Margate
9 20 A2
ee Cl CT2 30 B5
er Ct CT2 30 A1
er Rd CT2 34 D1
er St CT13 29 F2
ermans Wharf,
hitstable CT5 9 F2
ermans Wharf,
ndwich CT13 29 F1
gerald Av CT6 11 H2
mary Av CT9 18 C4
roy Av, Broadstairs
10 21 F4
roy Av, Margate
9 20 A4
roy Av, Ramsgate
12 22 B6
roy Pl CT10 21 F4
roy Rd CT5 9 H1
gstaff Ct CT1 6 D5
mingo Dr CT6 12 B4
ets La CT2 30 D1
etwood Av CT6 12 A3
cher Rd CT5 10 A4
t Cotts CT7 16 D5
t Gro CT10 23 E3
t Ho CT9 3 E2
ra Rd CT11 25 F3
rence Av CT5 8 C5
rence Cotts CT11 4 A2
rence Ct CT9 20 B2
rence Rd CT11 4 A3
ds Hill CT12 26 C5
ds La CT12 26 C6
d Cl, Canterbury
4 37 B5
d Cl, Herne Bay
6 11 F2
d Hill CT3 13 H6
d Walk CT5 7 A4
doun Rd CT10 5 A3
dwich Gro CT10 20 D6
dwich Pl CT13 29 E3
dwich Rd CT2 32 D3
eland Av CT9 20 C3
eland Ct CT11 4 A4
eland Heights
10 23 H1
eland Park Ho
10 23 G1
eness Cl CT10 21 F2
ge Cl CT2 32 D3
ge Cotts CT10 5 C2
ge La, Ramsgate
11 24 D3
ge La, Whitstable
5 9 E4
gefields CT6 14 D1
rester Cl CT1 32 A6
t Cotts CT10 5 D3
t Cres CT9 3 D1
t Hill CT9 3 D1
t Lwr CT9 3 E1
t Paragon CT9 3 E1
t Prom CT9 3 E1
t Rd, Broadstairs
10 5 D3
t Rd, Margate CT9 3 D2
tuna Ct CT11 25 E3
ty Acres Rd CT2 31 E6
sters Av CT10 20 D6
sters Ct CT13 29 E3
untain Inn Ct CT9 3 D2
untain St*, Harbour St
5 9 E1

Fountain St*, St Peters St
CT5 9 F2
Fox Dene Rd CT5 8 B5
Foxborough Cl
CT13 28 A5
Foxborough Hill C
CT13 28 A4
Foxborough La CT12 15 B5
Foxdown Cl CT2 31 E6
Foxgrove Rd CT5 9 H2
Foxs Cross Hill CT5 7 A3
Foxs Cross Rd CT5 7 B3
Frances Gdns CT11 25 G3
Francis Cl CT12 26 B6
Francis Rd CT10 23 G1
Franciscan Way CT1 6 A3
Franklyn Rd CT2 34 C2
Freda Cl CT10 25 G1
Freeman Ct CT1 31 H5
Freemans Cl CT5 8 B6
Freemans Rd CT12 15 B5
Frencham Cl CT2 31 G4
Freshlands CT6 13 G1
Freshwater Cl CT6 11 G3
Friars Cl CT5 9 G2
Friary Way CT2 30 D6
Friendly Cl CT9 20 C4
Friends Av CT9 20 C5
Friends Gap CT9 20 D2
Frost Cotts CT13 28 A4
Fulham Av CT9 18 D5
Fullers Yd CT9 3 E3
Fulmar Way CT6 13 H2
Fulsam Pl CT9 3 A4

Gainsboro Rd CT7 16 D2
Gainsborough Av
CT9 20 C5
Gainsborough Dr
CT6 13 G2
Galliard St CT13 29 F2
Gallwey Av CT7 16 C3
Gammons Yd CT2 6 B2
Gann Rd CT5 9 G2
Garden Cl CT2 30 B6
Gardeners Pl CT4 39 D3
Gardens Cl CT3 27 C2
Garfield Rd CT9 3 A4
Garrard Av CT9 18 D4
Gas Pass CT1 6 A5
Gas St CT1 6 A5
Gate Quays CT9 3 C3
Gateacre Rd CT5 8 B5
Gateway Ct CT11 4 F1
Genesta Av CT5 8 C4
Geoffrey Ct CT7 17 E3
George Hill Rd
CT10 20 D4
George Pk CT9 18 D4
George Roche Rd
CT1 35 F4
George St CT11 4 C2
George V Av CT9 18 D4
George Warren Ct
CT9 3 D4
Georges Av CT5 8 C5
Gilbert Rd CT11 25 E3
Gilbert Way CT1 35 E4
Gilchrist Av CT6 11 H4
Giles Gdns CT9 19 G4
Giles La CT2 30 C5
Gillon Mews CT1 31 H6
Gladstone Rd, Broadstairs
CT10 5 A3
Gladstone Rd, Margate
CT9 19 G4
Gladstone Rd, Whitstable
CT5 9 E2
Glebe Ct CT12 15 B6
Glebe Gdns CT9 18 C5
Glebe Rd CT9 18 C5
Glebe Way CT5 9 E4
Glebelands CT3 27 B2
Glen Av CT6 13 E2
Glen Iris Av CT2 30 C6
Glen Iris Cl CT2 30 C6
Glen Walk CT5 7 A3
Glenavon Ho CT10 23 G1
Glenbervie Dr CT6 13 G1
Glenbrook Cl CT6 13 F2
Glencoe Rd CT9 19 H3
Glenside CT5 9 H4
Glenside Av CT1 31 H6
Gloucester Av, Broadstairs
CT10 23 E5
Gloucester Av, Margate
CT9 20 C3
Gloucester Rd CT5 9 G2
Godden Rd CT2 31 G4

Godwin Rd, Canterbury
CT1 34 C4
Godwin Rd, Margate
CT9 20 A3
Goldcrest Walk CT5 8 C6
Golden Acre La CT8 17 H3
Golden Cl CT8 17 H3
Golden Hill CT5 9 G5
Goldfinch Cl CT6 13 E4
Goodban Sq CT3 27 B2
Goodwin Av CT5 10 C3
Goodwin Ct CT11 4 E1
Goodwin Pk CT9 22 A2
Goodwin Rd CT11 24 C5
Gordon Gro CT8 18 A4
Gordon Rd, Canterbury
CT1 6 A5
Gordon Rd, Herne Bay
CT6 12 C3
Gordon Rd, Margate
CT9 19 H2
Gordon Rd, Ramsgate
CT11 25 E2
Gordon Rd, Westwood
CT9 22 A3
Gordon Rd, Whitstable
CT5 9 E4
Gordon Sq CT7 16 D3
Gore Cl CT13 27 B5
Gore End Cl CT7 16 C3
Gore La CT13 27 B5
Gore Mews CT1 31 H6
Gore Rd CT13 27 B5
Gore Ter CT13 27 B5
Goretop La CT14 29 G5
Gorrell Ct CT5 9 F3
Gorrell Rd CT5 9 F3
Gorse La CT6 13 E5
Gosfield Rd CT6 12 C2
Gosselin St CT5 9 F4
Goudhurst Cl CT2 31 G4
Grafton Rd CT10 21 E6
Grafton Rise CT6 11 H2
Granary Pl CT5 9 E5
Grand Dr CT6 11 G1
Grand Mansions
CT10 5 C5
Grange Ct CT11 4 A3
Grange Rd, Broadstairs
CT10 23 E1
Grange Rd, Herne Bay
CT6 13 E3
Grange Rd, Ramsgate
CT11 4 A4
Grange Way CT10 23 E6
Grant Cl CT10 23 E2
Granville Av, Broadstairs
CT10 5 C5
Granville Av, Ramsgate
CT12 24 C1
Granville Ct CT11 4 F1
Granville Dr CT6 11 G4
Granville Farm Mews
CT11 25 G3
Granville Ho CT11 4 F1
Granville Rd CT10 5 B5
Grasmere Av CT11 24 B4
Grasmere Pk CT3 10 A6
Grasmere Rd CT5 9 H3
Grays Way CT1 34 C4
Graystone Rd CT5 9 H1
Great Stour Mws CT1 6 A4
Great Stour Pl CT2 6 B1
Green Acres Cl CT6 12 D4
Green Cloth Mews
CT1 31 H6
Green Ct CT4 37 B5
Green Dell CT2 31 F4
Green La, Broadstairs
CT10 23 E3
Green La, Margate
CT9 20 D5
Green La, Whitstable
CT5 9 E4
Green Leas CT5 10 C5
Green Rd CT7 16 D2
Greenbridge Pk CT1 32 A4
Greenfield Cotts CT1 6 A6
Greenfield Rd CT12 22 C6
Greenhill Bridge Rd
CT6 11 H2
Greenhill Cl CT12 15 B4
Greenhill Gdns CT12 15 B5
Greenhill Rd CT6 11 G4
Greenhouse La CT2 31 E6
Greenside Ho CT8 18 D3
Grenham Bay Av
CT7 16 C3

Grenham Bay Ct
CT7 16 D2
Grenham Rd CT7 16 C2
Grenville Gdns CT7 16 C2
Grenville Way CT10 23 E4
Gresham Av CT9 18 C4
Greyfriars Ct CT10 21 E4
Greystones Rd
CT12 26 B5
Grimshill Ct CT2 30 C4
Grimshill Rd CT5 9 F4
Grimthorpe Av CT5 8 D5
Grinan Ct CT11 25 G1
Grinsell Hill CT12 15 D5
Grosvenor Gdns CT9 3 D4
Grosvenor Hill CT9 3 D3
Grosvenor Pl CT9 3 C3
Grosvenor Rd, Broadstairs
CT10 5 A4
Grosvenor Rd, Ramsgate
CT11 24 D4
Grosvenor Rd, Whitstable
CT5 9 E5
Grotto Gdns CT9 3 F3
Grotto Hill CT9 3 F3
Grotto Rd CT9 3 F2
Grove Gdns CT9 18 D4
Grove Manor CT13 28 B5
Grove Rd CT11 4 B2
Grove Ter CT1 6 A6
Grummock Av CT11 24 C4
Grundys Hill CT11 4 C2
Guestling Mill Ct
CT13 29 E1
Guildcount La CT13 29 E1
Guildford Av CT8 17 H3
Guildford Lawn CT11 4 C2
Guildford Rd CT1 35 F3
Guildhall St CT1 6 C3
Guilton CT3 27 A2
Guy Cl CT10 23 G1
Gwyn Rd CT12 22 C6

Hackington Cl CT2 31 E4
Hackington Pl CT2 31 F6
Hackington Rd CT2 31 E2
Hackington Ter CT2 31 F6
Hadleigh Gdns CT6 12 D2
Hadlow Dr CT9 21 E3
Haine Ind Est CT12 24 B2
Haine Rd CT12 22 A4
Hales Dr CT2 31 F5
Halfmile Ride CT9 19 F6
Halford Cl CT6 13 E5
Hall Place Enterprise Centre
CT2 34 B1
Hall-by-the-Sea Rd
CT9 3 B3
Hallcroft Ct CT11 24 D4
Hallett Walk CT1 31 H6
Halstead Cl CT2 31 G4
Halstead Gdns CT9 21 E3
Ham Shades La CT5 9 H3
Hamill Ter CT1 31 H5
Hamilton Cl, Ramsgate
CT12 24 B1
Hamilton Cl, Broadstairs
CT10 23 G2
Hamilton Ct CT7 16 D5
Hamilton Rd CT5 9 F2
Hampshire Rd CT1 36 B3
Hampton Cl CT6 11 F3
Hampton Gdns CT6 11 F3
Hampton Heights
CT6 11 G1
Hampton Pier Av
CT6 11 G2
Hanover Cl CT9 20 D3
Hanover Pl CT2 31 F6
Hanover Sq CT6 12 C2
Hanover St CT6 12 B2
Hansard Ct CT8 18 C4
Hanscomb Ho CT2 31 E6
Harbledown By-Pass
CT2 34 A1
Harbledown Gdns
CT9 20 D2
Harbledown Pk CT2 34 C1
Harbledown Ter CT2 34 C1
Harbour Mws, Whitstable
CT5 9 E2
Harbour Mws, Broadstairs
CT10 5 C3
Harbour Par CT11 4 D2
Harbour St, Broadstairs
CT10 5 D3
Harbour St, Ramsgate
CT11 4 D2

Harbour St, Whitstable
CT5 9 E2
Harbour Twrs CT11 4 C3
Harcourt Dr, Canterbury
CT2 30 D6
Harcourt Dr, Herne Bay
CT6 11 G1
Hardres Rd CT11 25 F3
Hardres St CT11 4 D1
Hardy Cl CT2 34 D1
Harebrook CT11 25 G2
Harkness Dr CT2 30 D6
Harmsworth Gdns
CT10 5 A1
Harnet St CT13 29 E2
Harnwood Rd CT6 12 D5
Harold Av CT8 18 A4
Harold Rd, Birchington
CT7 16 B2
Harold Rd, Margate
CT9 20 A3
Harriets Cnr CT5 7 B2
Harrington Cl CT6 12 D4
Harrison Rd CT11 4 A3
Harrow Dene CT10 23 E3
Harry Wells Rd CT6 11 G2
Hartsdown Rd CT9 19 E3
Harty Ferry Vw CT5 8 D6
Harvest Ct CT6 13 F5
Harvey Dr CT5 10 A5
Harwich St CT5 9 E4
Hassall Reach CT1 34 B4
Hastings Av CT9 19 H3
Hastings Pl CT13 29 E3
Hatch La CT4 39 C1
Hatfield Rd, Margate
CT9 3 A3
Hatfield Rd, Ramsgate
CT11 4 A1
Havelock Pl CT3 27 C2
Havelock St CT1 6 D3
Haven Dr CT6 13 H1
Hawe Cl CT2 31 G4
Hawe Farm Way CT6 12 D5
Hawes Av CT11 24 C4
Hawk Cl CT5 8 D5
Hawkhurst Cl CT7 17 E2
Hawkhurst Way
CT10 23 G6
Hawks La CT1 6 B4
Hawks Rd CT6 11 G4
Hawley Sq CT9 3 D3
Hawley St CT9 3 D2
Hawthorn Av CT2 31 G5
Hawthorn Cl CT11 25 E1
Hawthorns CT7 17 H5
Hay Hill CT13 27 D6
Hazel Ct CT3 38 A5
Hazelmere Dr CT6 13 F1
Hazelwood Mdw
CT13 29 E3
Hazlemere Rd CT5 8 B5
Headcorn Dr CT2 31 G3
Headcorn Gdns CT9 20 D3
Heart in Hand Rd
CT6 13 H5
Heath Cl CT2 32 C1
Heather Cl CT9 19 E4
Heathwood Dr CT11 25 F1
Heaton Rd CT1 35 E3
Hedgend Ind Est
CT7 14 B4
Helding Cl CT6 13 E4
Helena Av CT9 19 G4
Helmdon Cl CT12 22 C6
Helvellyn Av CT11 24 C3
Hengist Av CT9 20 A4
Hengist Rd, Birchington
CT7 16 B3
Hengist Rd,
Westgate-on-Sea
CT8 17 G2
Henry Ct CT1 6 B6
Herbert Rd CT11 24 D4
Hereford Gdns CT7 16 D4
Hereson Rd CT11 25 F3
Hereward Av CT7 16 C2
Heritage Cl CT5 8 B6
Heritage Ct CT1 6 B4
Heritage Ho CT1 6 B4
Herne Av CT6 12 D3
Herne Bay Rd, Canterbury
CT2 32 C1
Herne Bay Rd, Whitstable
CT5 10 A3
Herne Bay West Ind Est
CT6 11 G3
Herne Dr CT6 11 H3
Herne St CT6 12 C6

Herneville Gdns CT6 12 D3
Heronden Rd CT13 27 A6
Heronden View CT13 27 A6
Herschell Rd CT7 16 D2
Hertford Ct CT1 36 A2
Hertford Ho CT6 12 D2
Hertford Pl CT11 4 C3
Hertford Rd CT9 20 B5
Hertford St CT11 4 C3
Hever Pl CT2 31 G5
Hibernia St CT11 4 D2
High St, Bridge CT4 37 A4
High St, Broadstairs CT10 5 A3
High St, Eastry CT13 27 B5
High St,Fordwich CT2 32 D4
High St, Garlinge CT9 18 C5
High St, Herne Bay CT6 12 B2
High St, Littlebourne CT3 38 A2
High St, Manston CT12 26 D3
High St, Margate CT9 3 C2
High St, Minster CT12 15 B5
High St, Northgate CT1 6 D2
High St, Ramsgate CT11 4 C1
High St, Sandwich CT13 29 F2
High St, St Georges CT1 6 B3
High St, St Lawrence CT11 24 C4
High St, St Peters CT10 23 E3
High St, Sturry CT2 32 D3
High St, Whitstable CT5 9 E2
High View Av CT6 11 G1
Higham Court Cotts CT4 37 C6
Higham La CT4 37 C6
Highbury Gdns CT12 22 B5
Highfield Cl, Canterbury CT2 30 C5
Highfield Cl, Ramsgate CT12 22 B5
Highfield Ct CT6 12 B2
Highfield Ct*, Highfield Cl CT12 22 B6
Highfield Gdns CT9 3 A4
Highfield Rd CT12 22 B5
Highfields Av CT6 13 F2
Highfields Vw CT6 13 F2
Highgate Pk CT5 10 B4
Highgate Rd CT5 10 A5
Highland Rd CT4 39 B3
Hilary Cl CT6 13 F2
Hildersham Cl CT10 23 E2
Hill Dr CT13 27 C5
Hill House Dr CT12 15 B4
Hill Rd CT13 28 A4
Hill Top Rd CT6 12 D2
Hillborough Dr CT6 13 H1
Hillborough Rd CT6 13 E2
Hillbrow Av, Canterbury CT2 32 D1
Hillbrow Av, Herne Bay CT6 12 D4
Hillbrow Rd CT11 25 E2
Hillcrest Gdns CT11 24 C4
Hillcrest Rd CT3 38 A2
Hillcroft Rd CT6 12 D4
Hiller Cl CT10 23 F2
Hillman Av CT6 11 F2
Hills Court Rd CT3 27 D2
Hills Ct CT3 27 D1
Hillside Av CT2 30 C6
Hillside Cotts CT4 37 D1
Hillside Pl CT4 39 D3
Hillside Rd CT5 9 H3
Hilltop CT5 9 E5
Hillview Rd, Canterbury CT2 30 C6
Hillview Rd, Whitstable CT5 9 E4
Hinchliffe Way CT9 20 C5
Hoades Wood Rd CT2 33 E1
Hobart Rd CT12 24 B1
Hockeredge Gdns CT9 18 B4
Hodges Gap CT9 20 B2
Hodgson Rd CT5 8 A5
Hogarth Cl CT6 13 G2
Hogs Cnr CT13 29 F2
Holbourn Cl CT6 14 D1
Holbrook Dr CT12 24 C1
Holiday Sq CT9 3 D2
Holland Cl CT10 21 G4
Hollicondane Rd CT11 25 E3
Hollow La CT1 35 E4
Hollowmede CT1 35 E4
Holly Cl CT10 22 C4
Holly Gdns CT9 20 C4
Holly La CT9 20 B3
Holly Rd CT11 25 F2
Hollytree Ctts CT4 37 D1
Holm Oak Cl CT1 35 F4
Holm Oak Gdns CT10 23 F4
Holman Mws CT1 6 C5
Holmes Way CT12 22 A5
Holmscroft Rd CT6 13 F2
Holness Rd CT3 27 B1
Holters Mill CT2 31 F6
Holton Cl CT7 17 E5
Holy Ghost Alley*, St Peters St CT13 29 F2
Homefern Ho CT9 3 D2
Homefleet Ho CT11 4 F1
Homeleigh Rd CT12 22 B5
Homersham CT1 34 D4
Homespire Ho CT1 6 C2
Homestall Ct CT2 30 C4
Homestead Cl CT9 19 G4
Homestead Village CT11 24 D5
Homewood Rd CT2 32 D2
Honeysuckle Cl CT9 19 E5
Honeysuckle Rd CT11 25 G3
Honeysuckle Way CT6 13 F4
Honeywood Cl CT1 31 H6
Honfleur Rd CT13 29 E2
Hoopers La CT6 13 F4
Hope Villas CT1 35 E4
Hopes La CT12 22 C5
Hopeville Av CT10 22 D2
Hornet Cl CT10 22 D4
Horsa Rd CT7 16 B3
Horsebridge Rd CT5 9 E2
Hoser Gdns CT7 17 E3
Hospital La CT1 6 B4
Hotham Ct CT1 31 H5
Hovenden Cl CT2 31 G4
Howard Rd CT10 5 A5
Howland Mews CT1 35 E4
Howletts Oast CT4 37 D1
Hubert Way CT10 23 E2
Hudson Cl CT2 32 D2
Hudson Rd CT1 31 H6
Hugin Av CT10 20 D6
Humber Av CT6 11 E2
Hundreds Cl CT8 17 H3
Hunters Chase, Herne Bay CT6 13 F5
Hunters Chase, Whitstable CT5 9 F5
Hunters Forstal Rd CT6 13 E5
Hunting Gate CT7 16 D3
Hunton Gdns CT2 31 G3
Hurst Gro CT12 24 D1
Hythe Pl CT13 29 F3

Ibis Cl CT5 9 E5
Iffin La CT1 35 E6
Ince Rd CT2 32 D1
Ingle Cl CT7 17 F3
Ingoldsby Rd, Birchington CT7 16 B3
Ingoldsby Rd, Canterbury CT1 34 D4
Inverary Ct CT11 25 F1
Inverness Ter CT10 5 B4
Invicta Ho, Margate CT9 20 B4
Invicta Ho, Canterbury CT1 6 C6
Invicta Rd, Margate CT9 20 B5
Invicta Rd, Whitstable CT5 9 G3
Irchester St CT11 4 E1
Iron Bar La CT1 6 C4
Irvine Dr CT9 20 C5
Irvine Mews CT9 20 C5
Island Rd, Hersden CT3 38 A6
Island Rd, Sturry CT2 32 D2
Island Wall CT5 8 D3
Ivanhoe Rd, Herne Bay CT6 12 D3
Ivanhoe Rd, Westgate-on-Sea CT8 18 A4
Ives Gate CT13 29 F1
Ivy Ct CT2 31 E1
Ivy House Rd CT5 9 G3
Ivy La, Canterbury CT1 6 D4
Ivy La, Ramsgate CT11 4 B3
Ivy Pl CT1 6 A6
Ivychurch Gdns CT9 21 E3
Ivyside CT8 18 A3

Jackson Rd CT1 35 E3
Jacob Cl CT9 19 F5
Jaffa Ct CT5 9 E3
James Cl CT3 27 B2
James St CT11 4 C3
Jasmine Cl CT4 39 C3
Jayne Walk CT5 8 C6
Jennifer Gdns CT9 20 C6
Jessica Mews*, Military Rd CT1 31 H6
Jesuit Cl CT2 31 G4
Jesus Hospital CT1 31 G6
Jewry La CT1 6 B3
Joanns Ct CT10 5 B3
John Nicholas Ho CT11 4 A3
John St CT10 5 C4
John Wilson Bsns Pk CT5 10 A4
Johns Grn CT13 28 D4
Joseph Conrad Ho CT2 34 D1
Joseph Conrad Ho*, Bishops Way CT2 34 D1
Joseph Wilson Ind Est CT5 9 H5
Joss Gap CT10 21 G5
Joss Gap Rd CT10 21 G4
Joy La CT5 8 B5
Jubilee Ct, Broadstairs CT10 5 C4
Jubilee Ct, Whitstable CT5 9 H1
Jubilee Rd, Canterbury CT3 38 A2
Jubilee Rd, Deal CT14 29 G6
Jubilee Rd, Sandwich CT13 29 E2
Julie Cl CT10 23 F1
Junction Rd CT6 11 G4
Juniper Cl, Canterbury CT1 35 G4
Juniper Cl, Whitstabl CT5 9 G3

Kain Ct CT12 24 C1
Kathryns Ct CT6 12 B2
Keat Farm Cl CT6 13 H2
Keats Crnr CT1 35 G4
Keats Pl CT9 3 F4
Keepers Hill CT4 37 D3
Keith Av CT12 24 B2
Kemp Rd CT5 10 B4
Kemsdale Ct CT2 30 C4
Kemsing Gdns CT2 31 H4
Kendal Cl CT11 24 C4
Kendal Mdw CT5 10 C4
Kendal Rise CT10 5 A1
Kennedy Ho CT11 4 E2
Kensington Rd CT1 32 A4
Kent & Canterbury Hospital CT1 35 G5
Kent Av CT1 36 A2
Kent Gdns CT7 16 D3
Kent Ho CT10 5 A4
Kent Pl CT11 4 E2
Kent Rd CT9 20 B5
Kent St CT5 9 E4
Kent Ter CT11 4 E2
Kentmere Av CT11 24 A4
Kenton Gdns CT12 15 B5
Kestrel Ct CT5 9 H1
Kevin Dr CT11 24 C5
Keyworth Mews CT1 31 H6
Kilbride Ct CT11 25 G1
Kilbride Ct*, Argyll Dr CT11 25 G1
Kilndown Gdns, Canterbury CT2 31 G4
Kilndown Gdns, Margate CT9 20 D3
Kimberley Ct CT8 18 A3
Kimberley Gro CT5 8 B6
Kimberley Rd CT12 24 B1
King Arthur Rd CT12 26 C4
King Edward Av, Broadstairs CT10 5 B4
King Edward Av, Herne Bay CT6 13 E2
King Edward Rd, Birchington CT7 16 D5
King Edward Rd, Ramsgate CT11 24 D4
King Edward St CT5 9 E3
King St, Canterbury CT1 6 C3
King St, Fordwich CT2 32 D4
King St, Margate CT9 3 D2
King St, Ramsgate CT11 4 D2
King St, Sandwich CT13 29 F2
Kingfisher Ct CT5 9 E4
Kingfisher Cl, Margate CT9 18 C5
Kingfisher Cl, Whitstable CT5 8 D5
Kingfisher Ct CT6 12 A4
Kingfisher Walk CT10 23 E3
Kings Av, Birchington CT7 16 B3
Kings Av, Broadstairs CT10 5 B1
Kings Av, Ramsgate CT12 24 C2
Kings Av, Whitstable CT5 9 G3
Kings Bri CT1 6 B3
Kings Mews CT1 6 D1
Kings Mws, Margate CT9 3 E2
Kings Mws, Ramsgate CT11 4 A2
Kings Pk CT1 35 H1
Kings Pl CT11 4 D2
Kings Rd, Birchington CT7 17 E5
Kings Rd, Herne Bay CT6 12 B2
Kings Rd, Ramsgate CT11 25 E3
Kingsdown Pk CT5 9 G1
Kingsfield Rd CT6 13 E4
Kingsgate Av CT10 21 E4
Kingsgate Bay Rd CT10 21 G3
Kingsgate Ct CT10 21 F3
Kingsley Rd CT5 9 F4
Kingsmead CT8 18 A3
Kingsmead Rd CT1 6 D1
Kingsmill Arc CT1 6 C2
Kingston Av CT9 18 D5
Kingston Cl, Herne Bay CT6 13 H2
Kingston Cl, Ramsgate CT12 24 C1
Kirbys Heights CT2 6 A1
Kirbys La CT2 6 A2
Kirkstone Av CT11 24 A4
Kite Fm CT5 10 C2
Kittiwake Cl CT6 13 H2
Knell La CT3 27 B1
Knight Av CT2 34 C2
Knightrider St CT13 29 F2
Knights Av CT10 5 C1
Knockholt Rd CT9 21 E2
Knold Pk CT9 19 F5
Knotts La CT1 6 C2
Knowler Way CT6 13 F2
Knowlton Walk CT1 31 H6

La Belle Alliance Sq CT11 4 E1
Laburnum Av CT13 29 E3
Laburnum La CT2 33 E1
Lady Woottons Grn CT1 6 D3
Ladyfields CT6 13 F5
Ladysmith Gro CT5 8 B6
Ladysmith Rd CT5 7 C2
Lagos Av CT12 24 B2
Lakeview International Bsns Pk CT3 38 D5
Laking Av CT10 23 G1
Laleham Gdns CT9 20 B4
Laleham Rd CT9 2
Laleham Walk CT9 2
Lamberhurst Way CT9 2
Lambeth Rd CT1 3
Lambourne Walk*, Russett Rd CT1 3
Lambs Walk CT5
Laming Rd CT7 1
Lancaster Cl CT12 2
Lancaster Gdns, Birching CT7 1
Lancaster Gdns, Herne B CT6 1
Lancaster Rd CT1 3
Lancet Dr CT6 1
Lanchester Cl CT6 1
Landon Rd CT6 1
Lane End CT6 1
Lanfrac Ho CT1
Lanfranc Gdns CT2 3
Lang Ct CT5 1
Langdale Av CT11 2
Langdon Av CT3 2
Langham Cl CT9 1
Langley Gdns CT9 2
Langton Gdns CT1
Langton Gdns*, Whitefriars St CT1 6
Langton La CT1 35
Lanhome Ct CT10 2
Lansdown Rd CT1
Lanthorne Rd CT10 2
Larch Cl, Broadstairs CT10 22
Larch Cl, Hersden CT3 3
Larkey Vw CT4 3
Larkscliff Ct CT7 1
Latimer Cl CT6 1
Laundry Rd CT12 15
Laureate Cl CT9 2
Laurel Way CT4 3
Laurensfield CT12 15
Laurice Ct CT11 24
Lauries Way*, Filmer Rd CT4 37
Lauriston Cl CT11 24
Lauriston Mt CT10
Lausanne Rd CT9
Lavender Cl, Margate CT9 1
Lavender Cl, Whitstable CT5 1
Lavender La CT12 2
Lavender Mews CT1 6
Law Cl CT2 34
Lawley Cl CT12 24
Lawn Rd CT10 5
Lawn Villas CT11 4
Lawrence Gdns CT6 13
Lawson Cl CT4 39
Laxton Way, Canterbury CT1 36
Laxton Way, Whitstable CT5 10
Lay La CT3 27
Laylam Cl CT10 22
Leander Ct CT5 9
Leas Grn CT10 22
Leatt Cl CT10 23
Leggetts La*, Sea St CT5 9
Leicester Av CT9 20
Leigh Rd CT12 24
Leighville Dr CT6 12
Lenham Cl CT10 23
Lenham Gdns CT9 18
Leona Ct CT9 20
Leonards Av CT11 25
Leopold Rd CT11 25
Leopold St CT11 4
Lerryn Gdns CT10 21
Lesley Av CT1 35
Leslie Av CT9 18
Leslie Rd CT7 17
Lewis Cres CT9 20
Leybourn Rd CT10 5
Leybourne Dr CT9 18
Leycroft Cl CT2 31
Leysdown Vw CT5 8
Library Rd CT2 31
Lichfield Av CT1 35
Lillian Rd CT11 25
Lime Cl CT4 39
Lime Gro CT11 4
Lime Kiln Rd CT1 6
Lincoln Av CT1 35
Lincoln Cl CT5 10

:oln Gdns CT7 16 D3
den Av, Broadstairs
'10 5 C1
den Av, Herne Bay
'6 12 A3
den Av, Whitstable
'5 9 G3
den Chase CT2 6 A2
den Cl CT8 18 A5
den Gro CT2 6 A2
den Rd, Canterbury
'4 39 D3
den Rd,
estgate-on-Sea
'8 18 A5
denthorpe Rd
'10 5 A1
dridge Cl CT6 14 D1
en Ct CT1 6 B4
ngton Rd CT7 17 E4
k La CT1 6 C4
k Rd,
oadstairs CT10 21 E6
k Rd, Sturry CT2 32 D1
k Rd, Tyler Hill
'2 31 E2
ks Cl CT6 12 D4
ksfield Rd CT8 17 H3
ey Rd CT10 21 E6
net Av CT5 8 D6
nard Ho CT2 35 E1
a Ct CT5 9 H1
nore Rd, Herne Bay
'6 13 F1
nore Rd, Whitstable
'5 10 A6
s Rd CT13 27 A6
Mdws CT3 38 A2
er Ho CT9 19 H4
er Rd CT9 19 H4
e Charles St*,
arles St CT6 12 C1
e Copse Cl CT4 39 D3
e Court CT3 38 B2
e Paddocks CT5 10 C6
e Walton CT13 27 C5
ebourne Ct CT3 38 B1
ebourne Rd CT1 36 A2
erpool Lawn CT11 4 C3
ingstone Rd
T10 23 E2
yd Rd CT10 5 A3
dge Field Rd CT5 10 C5
mbard St CT9 3 D2
ndon Rd, Canterbury
T2 34 D1
ndon Rd, Ramsgate
T11 24 C4
ng Acre CT7 17 H6
ng Acre Cl CT2 31 E6
ng Dr CT13 27 C5
ng Meadow Way
T2 31 F4
ng Reach Cl CT5 9 E6
ng Rock CT5 10 C3
ngacre CT5 10 C5
ngfield Cl CT5 10 C3
ngfield Ct CT5 10 C3
ngmarket CT1 6 C4
ngmarket Sq CT1 6 C4
ngmead Cl CT6 11 H3
ngport CT1 6 D4
ngtail Rise CT6 12 A4
ngtye Dr CT5 10 B6
nsdale Av CT9 20 B2
nsdale Dr CT6 11 G1
op Court Mews
T13 29 E1
op St CT13 29 E2
rina Rd CT12 24 D2
rne Rd CT11 24 D4
ughborough Ct
T11 25 F3
uisa Gap CT10 5 C5
ve La, Canterbury
T1 6 D4
ve La, Margate
T9 3 D2
ve Street Cl CT6 11 H4
vell Rd CT2 30 B5
wer Bridge St CT1 6 D4
wer Chantry La
T1 35 G2
wer Dumpton Park Rd
T11 25 F2
wer Gore La CT13 27 B5
wer Herne Rd CT6 12 A6
wer Northdown Av
T9 20 A4

Lower St CT13 27 C6
Lucerne Dr CT5 8 A6
Luckhurst Gdns CT9 20 D3
Luton Av CT10 5 A5
Luton Ct CT10 5 A5
Lyell Ct CT7 16 D3
Lyell Rd CT7 16 D3
Lyminge Way CT9 20 B4
Lymington Cl CT8 18 A5
Lymington Rd CT8 17 H3
Lyndhurst Av CT9 20 A3
Lyndhurst Cl CT2 31 E5
Lyndhurst Rd, Broadstairs
CT10 5 B1
Lyndhurst Rd, Ramsgate
CT11 25 G3
Lyngate Ct CT9 20 D3
Lypeatt Ct CT2 30 C3
Lysander Cl CT10 22 C5
Lytham Av CT6 12 A5

Macdonald Par CT5 8 B5
Madeira Rd CT9 19 H2
Madeira Walk CT11 4 D2
Magdala Rd CT10 23 E2
Magdalen Ct, Broadstairs
CT10 5 B1
Magdalen Ct, Canterbury
CT1 35 G3
Magnolia Av CT9 20 C3
Magnolia Dr CT4 39 D3
Magnolia Rise CT6 13 F5
Maiden La CT1 34 D4
Major Cl CT5 8 C6
Malham Dr CT9 19 H4
Mallard Cl CT6 12 B4
Mallory Cl CT12 22 C6
Malthouse Rd CT2 31 F6
Malvern Pk CT6 13 F2
Manciple Cl CT2 34 C2
Mandarin La CT6 12 A4
Mandeville Rd CT2 31 E6
Manktelow Ct CT10 23 F6
Manor Barns CT13 28 B5
Manor Cl CT1 34 C5
Manor Ct CT1 6 B6
Manor Dr CT7 16 D4
Manor End CT7 14 C6
Manor Lea Rd CT7 14 C6
Manor Rd, Broadstairs
CT10 5 A4
Manor Rd, Herne Bay
CT6 13 H1
Manor Rd, St Nicholas at
Wade CT7 14 B5
Manor Rd, Whitstable
CT5 9 H1
Mansion St CT9 3 D2
Manston Court Rd, Margate
CT9 22 A4
Manston Court Rd,
Ramsgate CT12 26 C2
Manston Ct CT12 26 C1
Manston Pk CT12 15 C2
Manston Rd, Birchington
CT7 17 E6
Manston Rd, Manston
CT12 26 A1
Manston Rd, Margate
CT9 19 F6
Manston Rd, Ramsgate
CT11,12 24 A2
Manswood Hospital
CT2 31 F5
Manwood Av CT2 31 F4
Manwood Rd CT13 29 F3
Maple Cl, Canterbury
CT2 30 B5
Maple Cl, Margate
CT9 21 E4
Maple Ct CT3 38 B5
Maple Gdns CT3 38 B5
Maple Ho CT2 30 B5
Marden Av CT12 24 C3
Margate Hill CT7 17 G6
Margate Rd, Broadstairs
CT10 22 A3
Margate Rd, Herne Bay
CT6 13 E4
Margate Rd, Ramsgate
CT12 24 D1
Marilyn Cres CT7 17 F3
Marina Esp CT11 4 E2
Marina Rd CT11 4 F1
Marine Cres CT5 10 A3
Marine Ct CT5 9 G1
Marine Dr, Broadstairs
CT10 21 F3

Marine Dr, Margate
CT9 3 C3
Marine Gap CT5 9 E2
Marine Gdns CT9 3 C3
Marine Heights CT8 18 A3
Marine Par CT5 9 G1
Marine Ter, Margate
CT9 3 B3
Marine Ter, Whitstable
CT5 8 D2
Mariners Ct CT5 9 E3
Mariners Lea, Broadstairs
CT10 22 D4
Mariners Lea, Whitstable
CT5 9 F1
Maritime Av CT6 13 E3
Mark Av CT11 24 C5
Market Pl CT9 3 D2
Market St, Herne Bay
CT6 12 B1
Market St, Margate
CT9 3 D2
Market St, Sandwich
CT13 29 F2
Market Way CT2 31 G6
Marlborough Cl
CT10 23 E5
Marlborough Rd, Margate
CT9 19 F4
Marlborough Rd,
Ramsgate CT11 4 B2
Marlborough Rd, Whitstable
CT5 7 D1
Marley Ct CT2 30 C4
Marlow Cl CT5 10 A4
Marlowe Arc CT1 6 C4
Marlowe Av CT1 6 B5
Marlowe Ct CT1 6 B5
Marlowe Mdws CT2 32 D3
Marlowe Rd CT9 20 B5
Marrose Av CT12 22 B5
Marsh Farm Rd
CT12 15 B6
Marshall Cres CT10 23 E4
Marshborough Rd
CT13 28 A3
Marshwood Cl CT1 32 A5
Martindale Cl CT1 35 G3
Martindown Rd CT5 8 D5
Martins Cl CT12 24 D1
Martony Ct CT9 3 E2
Martyrs Field Rd CT1 6 A6
Mary Green Walk
CT1 31 H6
Maryland Gro CT1 35 H4
Masons Rise CT10 5 A2
Matador Dr CT6 13 E4
Mathew Ct CT2 6 A2
Matthews Rd CT6 11 H4
Maudslay Cl CT6 12 D4
Maugham Ct CT5 9 E4
Maxine Gdns CT10 23 E3
Maxted Ct CT6 13 F2
May St CT6 13 H3
Maybrook Ind Est
CT1 32 A4
Maydowns Rd CT5 10 C4
Mayfield Rd CT6 12 C3
Mayforth Rd CT11 24 C5
Maymills Cotts CT13 27 B6
Maynard Av CT9 18 D5
Maynard Rd CT1 35 E3
Mays Rd CT11 24 D4
Maystreet CT6 13 H3
Mayville Rd CT10 23 E2
McCarthy Av CT2 32 D1
McKinlay Ct CT7 16 B2
Mead Way CT2 35 E1
Meadow Cl, Canterbury
CT4 37 C5
Meadow Cl, Herne Bay
CT6 13 E3
Meadow Ct CT9 20 A5
Meadow Dr CT5 10 C5
Meadow Rd, Canterbury
CT2 30 C6
Meadow Rd, Margate
CT9 18 C4
Meadow Rd, Sturry
CT2 32 D2
Meadow Walk CT5 8 D5
Medina Av CT5 8 C5
Meeting Ct CT9 3 D2
Meeting St CT11 4 C1
Melbourne Av CT12 24 B2
Mellanby Cl CT7 17 E4
Mellington Gdns CT9 3 E2
Melloy Mws CT9 3 E1
Melsetter Cl CT7 17 F3

Melville Lea CT13 28 B4
Memel Pl CT11 4 B2
Mentmore Ho CT12 22 C5
Mentmore Rd CT12 22 C5
Mercery La CT1 6 C3
Merchants Way CT2 34 C2
Mere Gate CT9 19 F4
Merrivale Heights
CT10 5 B6
Merrywood Gro CT6 13 F5
Merton La CT1 35 E6
Metcalfe Mews CT1 31 H6
Meteor Av CT5 8 C4
Meverall Av CT12 26 C5
Michael Av CT11 25 G2
Michelle Gdns CT9 18 B4
Mickleburgh Av CT6 12 D3
Mickleburgh Hill CT6 12 C2
Middle Wall CT5 9 E2
Mildmay Ct CT11 4 F1
Miles Way CT7 16 D3
Military Rd, Canterbury
CT1 6 D2
Military Rd, Ramsgate
CT11 4 C3
Mill Bank CT13 27 A6
Mill Cl CT13 28 D1
Mill Cotts CT11 4 A3
Mill Court Cl CT6 12 D5
Mill Fld, Broadstairs
CT10 23 F2
Mill Fld, Canterbury
CT3 27 D3
Mill Grn CT13 27 B6
Mill La, Birchington
CT7 16 D4
Mill La, Bridge CT4 37 A5
Mill La, Canterbury
CT1 6 C2
Mill La, Harbledown
CT2 34 C2
Mill La, Herne Bay
CT6 12 D5
Mill La, Margate CT9 3 D3
Mill La, Ramsgate
CT12 22 B5
Mill La, Eastry CT13 27 A6
Mill La, Sandwich
CT13 29 F6
Mill La North CT6 13 E4
Mill Rd CT2 32 C3
Mill Row CT7 16 D4
Mill Ter, Bridge CT4 37 A5
Mill Ter, Chartham
CT4 39 C1
Mill View Rd CT6 12 C5
Millennium Ter CT1 34 C4
Millennium Way
CT10 22 B4
Miller Av CT2 34 D1
Millers Ct, Whitstable
CT5 9 E5
Millers Ct, Ramsgate
CT12 24 C1
Millers Yd CT1 6 A6
Millfield Manor CT5 9 F3
Millfield Rd CT12 22 B5
Millmead Av CT9 20 C5
Millmead Gdns CT9 20 C5
Millmead Rd CT9 20 A4
Millstream Cl CT5 9 F3
Millstrood Rd CT5 9 F3
Millwall Pl CT13 29 F2
Milner La CT2 32 C3
Milner Rd CT5 8 B6
Milton Av CT9 3 E4
Milton Cl CT1 36 A4
Milton Rd CT1 35 G4
Milton Sq CT9 3 E4
Mindora Heights
CT2 34 C2
Miners Way CT3 38 D5
Minnis Rd CT7 16 B2
Minnis Way CT14 29 G6
Minster Cl CT10 23 G6
Minster Dr CT6 12 A2
Minster Lodge CT11 24 D4
Minster Rd, Minster
CT12 15 B1
Minster Rd, Ramsgate
CT11 24 C5
Minster Rd,
Westgate-on-Sea
CT8 18 A5
Moat Ho CT1 6 B6
Moat La, Ash CT3 27 C2
Moat La, Fordwich
CT2 32 D4

Moat La, Canterbury
CT2 30 B4
Moat Sole CT13 29 E2
Mockett Dr CT10 21 E6
Molehill Rd CT5 10 C6
Molineux Rd CT12 15 B6
Molland Cl CT3 27 B2
Molland La CT3 27 A2
Molland Lea CT3 27 B1
Monastery St CT1 6 D4
Monks Cl CT2 31 G5
Monkton Cotts CT11 4 C1
Monkton Ct CT5 10 C6
Monkton Gdns CT9 21 E2
Monkton Pl CT11 4 C1
Monkton Rd CT12 15 A5
Montague Rd CT11 25 F3
Montague St CT6 12 A2
Montefiore Av CT11 25 G1
Montefiore Cotts
CT11 25 G3
Montfort Cl CT2 31 G4
Montpelier Av CT5 7 D1
Moorfield CT2 31 F4
Moray Av CT7 16 D2
Mordaunt Av CT8 17 H2
Morden Cotts CT11 4 A2
Morris Av CT6 11 E2
Mortimer St CT6 12 B2
Moss End Mews
CT11 23 E6
Mount Charles Walk
CT4 37 A5
Mount Charles Walk*,
Union Rd CT4 37 A5
Mount Green Av
CT12 26 C6
Mount Pleasant CT2 30 A2
Mount Rd CT1 36 A4
Mount View Rd CT6 12 D5
Mountfield Mews
CT8 17 G4
Mountfield Way CT8 17 G4
Moyes Cl CT12 26 B5
Muir Rd CT11 25 G2
Mulberry Cl CT11 25 G3
Mulberry Ct CT1 6 B4
Mulberry Fld CT13 29 E1
Muscovy Way CT6 12 B4
Musgrave Cl CT12 26 A2
Mutrix Gdns CT9 18 C4
Mutrix Rd CT9 18 C4
Mymms Cl CT5 10 B6
Mystole La CT4 39 C3

Nacholt Cl CT5 9 H2
Nackington Ct CT1 35 H4
Nackington La CT1 35 G6
Nackington Rd CT1 35 H5
Napier Ct CT10 23 E2
Napier Rd CT10 23 E2
Napleton Ct CT11 24 D5
Napleton Rd CT11 24 D4
Nargate Cl CT3 38 B2
Nargate St CT3 38 B2
Nash Court Gdns
CT9 19 G5
Nash Court Rd CT9 19 G5
Nash Gdns CT10 5 C3
Nash La CT9 19 G5
Nash Rd, Margate
CT9 19 F5
Nash Rd, Westwood
CT9 22 A3
Nasmyth Rd CT7 17 E2
Naylands CT9 3 A4
Neals Place Rd CT2 30 C5
Neame Rd CT7 17 E3
Nelson Cres CT11 4 C3
Nelson Ct CT7 16 C3
Nelson Pl CT10 5 C2
Nelson Rd CT5 9 E3
Neptune Gap CT5 9 E2
Nethercourt Circus
CT11 24 C4
Nethercourt Farm Rd
CT11 24 C4
Nethercourt Gdns
CT11 24 C4
Nethercourt Hill
CT11 24 C4
Nethersole Cl CT2 31 G4
Neville Rd CT6 13 H2
New Cross St CT9 3 D2
New Dover Rd CT1 35 G3
New Haine Rd CT12 22 A5
New House Cl CT1 35 E6
New House La CT1 35 E6
New Rd CT2 30 A5

New Romney Pl CT13 29 E3
New Ruttington La CT1 6 D1
New St, Ash CT3 27 C2
New St, Canterbury CT1 6 A6
New St, Herne Bay CT6 12 C2
New St, Margate CT9 3 C2
New St, Sandwich CT13 29 F2
New St, St Dunstans CT2 35 E1
New St, Whitstable CT5 9 E1
New Town St CT2 31 G6
Newbury Cl CT7 17 F4
Newbys Pl CT9 3 D2
Newcastle Hill CT11 4 E1
Newgate Lower Prom CT9 3 F1
Newgate Prom CT9 3 F1
Newing Cl CT3 38 A2
Newington Ct CT12 24 C2
Newington Rd CT12 22 B6
Newlands Ho CT11 23 E6
Newlands La CT12 22 C5
Newlands Rd CT12 25 E1
Newmans Cl CT10 23 G2
Newport Cotts CT4 37 C1
Newport Ct CT1 35 H4
Newton Rd CT5 10 A4
Nicholas Dr CT12 26 C6
Nicholls Av CT10 23 F6
Nickle Ct CT2 30 C4
Nightingale Av CT5 8 C6
Nightingale Pl CT9 3 F2
Nightingale Rd CT6 14 B2
Nixon Av CT12 22 C6
No Name St*, New St CT13 29 F2
Noble Ct CT9 18 C4
Noble Gdns CT9 18 C5
Nonsuch Cl CT1 36 A2
Norfolk Rd, Canterbury CT1 35 E4
Norfolk Rd, Margate CT9 20 A2
Norfolk Sq CT12 24 C1
Norfolk St CT5 9 E4
Norman Rd, Broadstairs CT10 23 E2
Norman Rd, Canterbury CT1 6 C6
Norman Rd, Ramsgate CT11 24 C5
Norman Rd, Westgate-on-Sea CT8 18 B4
Norman Rd, Whitstable CT5 9 F4
Norrie Rd CT7 17 E4
North Av CT11 4 B2
North Ct CT12 22 B6
North Foreland Av CT10 21 G6
North Foreland Hill CT10 21 G5
North Foreland Rd CT10 21 G6
North Holmes Rd CT1 35 G1
North La CT2 6 A2
North St CT6 12 C1
North Vw CT3 38 C5
Northbourne Way CT9 20 D4
Northcliffe Gdns CT10 21 F6
Northdown Av CT9 20 A3
Northdown Hill CT10 20 D5
Northdown Park Rd CT9 20 A4
Northdown Rd, Broadstairs CT10 23 E1
Northdown Rd, Margate CT9 3 E2
Northdown Way CT9 20 C5
Northgate CT1 6 D2
Northumberland Av CT9 20 B4
Northwood Ho CT6 12 A5
Northwood Rd, Ramsgate CT12 22 C5
Northwood Rd, Whitstable CT5 9 F1
Norton Av CT6 14 D1
Norton Dr CT12 15 B5
Norview Rd CT5 8 D5
Notley St CT1 35 G1
Nottingham Rd CT7 16 D5
Nunnery Flds CT1 6 C6
Nunnery Rd CT1 6 C6
Nursery Cl, Ramsgate CT11 24 D3
Nursery Cl, Whitstable CT5 9 H3
Nursery Gdns CT9 21 E4
Nursery Walk CT2 31 E6
Nurserylands CT6 12 B4

Oak Hill CT13 28 A4
Oak Tree Gro CT9 18 C5
Oakdale Rd CT6 12 D3
Oakdene Rd CT12 24 D1
Oakfield Ct CT12 24 C2
Oakland Ct, Ramsgate CT12 26 B6
Oakland Ct, Herne Bay CT6 12 B2
Oaklands Av CT10 22 D3
Oaklands Way CT2 33 E1
Oakleigh La CT4 37 C1
Oakridge CT10 21 F4
Oaks Av CT6 11 H3
Oaks Pk CT2 30 B5
Oakwood CT9 20 C5
Oakwood Dr CT5 9 H2
Oakwood Ind Est CT10 22 D1
Oakwood Mews CT5 9 E5
Oakwood Rd CT2 33 E1
Oast Cotts CT13 28 B4
Oast Ct CT9 19 G4
Oaten Hill CT1 6 D6
Oaten Hill Ct CT1 6 D5
Oaten Hill Pl CT1 6 D5
Ocean Cl CT7 17 F2
Ocean Vw, Broadstairs CT10 25 H1
Ocean Vw, Herne Bay CT6 13 H1
Ocivan Way CT9 22 A3
Offley Cl CT9 20 C4
Ogilvy Ct CT10 20 D6
Olantigh Ct CT7 17 E3
Olave Rd CT9 20 A4
Old Boundary Rd CT9 18 B3
Old Bridge Rd CT5 9 F3
Old Church Way CT4 39 D3
Old Crossing Rd CT9 18 C4
Old Dairy Cl CT11 25 G3
Old Dairy Yd CT11 24 D4
Old Dover Rd CT1 6 C5
Old Farm Cl CT5 9 E6
Old Farm Rd CT7 16 B3
Old Fold CT5 10 B6
Old Garden Ct CT4 39 D3
Old Green Rd, Broadstairs CT10 21 E6
Old Green Rd, Margate CT9 20 B4
Old Hall Dr CT12 26 B5
Old Kingsdown Cl CT10 23 E5
Old Minster Rd CT12 15 B3
Old Park Av CT1 31 H5
Old Park Ct CT1 32 A5
Old Ruttington La CT1 6 D3
Old School Cl CT2 32 D2
Old School Gdns CT9 19 H4
Old School Mews CT4 39 A2
Old Timber Yd Ind Est CT12 24 A3
Old Vicarage Gdn CT2 32 D2
Old Watling St CT1 6 A4
Omer Av CT9 20 B3
Orange St CT1 6 C3
Orchard Cl, Canterbury CT2 31 F4
Orchard Cl, Littlebourne CT3 38 A3
Orchard Cl, Minster CT12 15 B4
Orchard Cl, Ramsgate CT12 22 B5
Orchard Cl, Whitstable CT5 9 G1
Orchard Ct CT6 12 C6
Orchard End CT11 24 B6
Orchard Flats CT1 36 B3
Orchard Gdns CT9 18 C4
Orchard Gro CT5 9 E4
Orchard Rd, Herne Bay CT6 12 C4
Orchard Rd, Margate CT9 18 C4
Orchard Rd, Sandwich CT13 27 B5
Orchard Row CT6 12 D6
Orchard St CT2 35 E1
Orchard Vw CT3 27 D3
Orchid Cotts CT1 34 C6
Orient Pl CT2 6 B1
Osborne Gdns CT6 13 F2
Osborne Rd CT10 23 F4
Osborne Ter CT9 3 E4
Osbourn Av CT8 17 H2
Osbourne Rd CT10 5 A4
Oscar Rd CT10 5 C4
Osprey Cl CT5 8 D5
Otham Cl CT2 31 G4
Owls Hatch Rd CT6 11 G5
Oxenden Park Dr CT6 12 A3
Oxenden Sq CT6 12 A2
Oxenden St CT6 12 A2
Oxford Ct CT1 6 B6
Oxford Rd CT1 35 F3
Oxford St, Margate CT9 3 E4
Oxford St, Whitstable CT5 9 E3
Oxney Cl CT7 16 D3
Oyster Cl CT6 11 G3
Oyster Mews*, Skinners Alley CT5 9 E3

Packers La CT11 4 D1
Paddock Rd CT7 17 E4
Paddock Vw CT5 9 F5
Paffard Cl CT2 32 D1
Pafford Ct CT2 32 D1
Pal Cres CT7 17 H6
Palace Cl CT5 10 A4
Palace St CT1 6 C3
Palm Bay Av CT9 20 B2
Palm Bay Gdns CT9 20 B2
Palm Ct CT8 17 H1
Palmars Cross Hill CT2 34 B1
Palmer Cl CT6 12 D6
Palmer Cres CT9 20 B5
Palmerston Av CT10 5 C5
Paradise CT11 4 B1
Paradise Row CT13 29 E1
Paragon Ct CT9 3 E1
Paragon Royal Par CT11 4 C4
Paragon St CT11 4 C4
Pardoner Cl CT2 34 C2
Parham Cl CT1 31 H6
Parham Ct CT1 31 H5
Parham Rd CT1 31 H5
Parish Cl CT10 23 E2
Parish Rd CT4 39 B2
Park Av, Birchington CT7 16 D4
Park Av, Broadstairs CT10 23 E6
Park Av, Whitstable CT5 9 G1
Park Chase CT10 23 E6
Park Cl CT9 20 C4
Park Crescent Rd CT9 3 F3
Park Farm Cl CT2 31 E2
Park Gate CT10 23 E6
Park La, Birchington CT7 17 E4
Park La, Margate CT9 3 F3
Park Pl, Herne Bay CT6 14 D1
Park Pl, Margate CT9 3 D3
Park Rd, Birchington CT7 17 E4
Park Rd, Broadstairs CT10 23 H2
Park Rd, Herne Bay CT6 12 B2
Park Rd, Margate CT9 3 F3
Park Rd, Ramsgate CT11 25 E3
Park Royal CT6 12 D3
Park Ter CT13 28 C4
Park Vw, Canterbury CT2 32 D1
Park Vw, Margate CT9 3 F3
Park Wood Cl CT10 25 F1
Park Wood Rd CT2 30 C3
Parkland Ct CT10 23 F2
Parkside Villas CT9 19 F4
Parkwood Cl CT10 23 E6
Parsonage Farm Rd CT13 28 A3
Parsonage Rd CT6 12 C4
Partridge Cl CT6 13 E4
Patricia Way CT10 22 C5
Patrixbourne Rd CT4 37 B5
Payton Cl CT9 19 H6
Payton Mews CT1 35 H1
Payton Mews*, Military Rd CT1 31 H6
Peak Dr CT13 27 B5
Pean Court Rd CT5 7 D3
Pean Hill CT5 7 E3
Pear Tree Cl CT10 22 C4
Pearmain Walk*, Russett Rd CT1 36 A2
Pearsons Way CT10 20 D6
Peartree Rd CT6 13 E4
Peelers Ct CT2 6 B1
Pegwell Av CT11 24 C6
Pegwell Cl CT11 24 B5
Pegwell Rd CT11 24 B6
Pembroke Av CT9 18 C3
Pengelly Pl CT2 31 F6
Penshurst Cl CT2 31 G5
Penshurst Gdns CT9 21 E3
Penshurst Rd CT11 25 G3
Percy Av CT10 21 E4
Percy Rd, Broadstairs CT10 5 A2
Percy Rd, Margate CT9 19 H1
Percy Rd, Ramsgate CT11 25 E3
Perkins Av CT9 19 G4
Petchell Mews*, Military Rd CT1 31 H6
Petrel Cl CT6 13 H2
Pett Hill CT4 37 A4
Pettman Cl CT6 12 C3
Petts Cres CT12 15 B6
Pewter Ct CT1 6 C6
Philip Corby Cl CT9 20 B3
Phillips Rd CT7 17 E4
Picton Rd CT11 24 D4
Pier App CT10 5 D3
Pier Av, Herne Bay CT6 12 A3
Pier Av, Whitstable CT5 9 H1
Pier Chine CT6 12 B2
Pier Yd CT11 4 E2
Pierpoint Rd CT5 9 E5
Pierremont Av CT10 5 B3
Pigeon La CT6 12 D4
Pilckem Cl CT1 36 B1
Pilgrims La CT5 7 B2
Pilgrims Rd CT1 36 A3
Pilgrims Way CT1 35 H2
Pillory Gate CT13 29 F1
Pillory Gate Wharf CT13 29 F1
Pin Hill CT1 6 A5
Pine Tree Av CT2 31 E6
Pine Walk CT6 13 H1
Pineside Rd CT3 38 A1
Pinetree Cl, Birchington CT7 17 E3
Pinetree Cl, Whitstable CT5 9 G1
Pinewood Cl CT12 24 D2
Pintail Way CT6 13 E4
Pioneer Bsns Pk CT12 24 D2
Pippin Av CT4 37 C6
Pippin Cl CT13 27 D2
Plains of Waterloo CT11 4 E1
Plantation Rd CT5 10 C4
Plaxton Wy CT6 12 D4
Plenty Brook Dr CT6 12 B4
Pleydell Cres CT2 32 D1
Plough Ct CT6 13 F4
Plough La CT5 10 C2
Plover Cl CT6 13 H2
Pluckley Gdns CT9 20 D3
Plum Tree Gro CT7 16 D3
Plumpton Walk*, Military Rd CT1 31 H6
Plumstone Rd CT12 15 A1
Pochard Cres CT6 12 A4
Poets Cnr CT9 19 H3
Poldark Ct CT11 4 F1
Pollard Pl CT5 8 D6
Polo Way CT5 10 C5
Pomfret Ho CT4 39
Pomfret Rd CT4 39
Pond Cotts CT6 13
Poorhole La CT10 22
Popes La CT2 32
Poplar Dr CT6 11
Poplar Rd, Broadstairs CT10 23
Poplar Rd, Ramsgate CT11 4
Poplar Row CT7 17
Portland Ct CT11 25
Portland Sq CT1 35
Portlight Pl CT5 8
Portway CT5 9
Post Ter CT5 9
Potten Street Rd CT7 14
Potter St CT13 29
Poulders Gdns CT13 28
Poulders Rd CT13 28
Poulton La CT3 27
Pound La CT1 6
Powell Cotton Dr CT7 17
Prestedge Av CT11 23
Preston Par CT5 8
Preston Rd CT12 26
Pretoria Rd CT1 35
Prices Av, Margate CT9 20
Prices Av, Ramsgate CT11 24
Priest Av CT2 34
Priest Flds CT6 13
Priest Walk CT5 10
Primrose Way, Ramsgate CT12 26
Primrose Way, Whitstable CT5 10
Prince Andrew Rd CT10 21
Prince Charles Rd CT10 20
Prince Edwards Prom CT11 24
Princes Av CT12 24
Princes Cl CT7 16
Princes Cres CT9 3
Princes Gdns CT9 20
Princes Rd CT11 25
Princes St, Margate CT9 3
Princes St, Ramsgate CT11 4
Princes Walk CT9 20
Princes Way CT2 35
Princess Anne Rd CT10 20
Princess Cl CT5 10
Princess Margaret Av, Margate CT9 20
Princess Margaret Av, Ramsgate CT12 24
Princess Rd CT5 10
Prioress Rd CT2 34
Priory Cl CT10 23
Priory Ctyd CT1 4
Priory Gdns CT1 35
Priory La CT6 12
Priory Mews CT11 4
Priory of St Jacob CT1 35
Priory Rd CT11 4
Promenade, Broadstairs CT10 5
Promenade, Margate CT9 3
Prospect Cl CT8 18
Prospect Gdns CT12 15
Prospect Hill CT6 12
Prospect Mws CT10 5
Prospect Pl, Broadstairs CT10 5
Prospect Pl, Canterbury CT1 35
Prospect Rd, Birchington CT7 16
Prospect Rd, Broadstairs CT10 5
Prospect Rd, Ramsgate CT12 15
Prospect Ter CT11 4
Providence Cotts CT11 24
Puckle La CT1 6
Pudding La CT3 27
Puffin Rd CT6 13
Pullman Cl CT12 24

ıp La CT9 3 D3
:has Ct CT2 30 C3
Alley La CT5 7 C3
tt Mews*, Military Rd 1 31 H6
ons Rd CT12 22 C6
ons Rd Ind Est 10 22 C5
ıntock Gdns CT12 22 B5
y Ct CT5 9 F2
y La CT13 29 F2
en Bertha Rd 11 24 D5
en Berthas Av 7 17 G3
en Elizabeth Av 9 20 C4
en Elizabeth Lodge 9 20 B3
en Elizabeth The Queen other Hospital CT9 19 G5
en St, Herne Bay 6 12 B2
en St, Ramsgate 11 4 C2
en Victoria Memorial sp CT6 13 E2
eens Av, Birchington 7 16 B3
eens Av, Broadstairs 10 5 C1
eens Av, Canterbury 2 34 D1
eens Av, Herne Bay 6 13 F2
eens Av, Margate 9 3 D4
eens Av, Ramsgate 12 24 C2
eens Ct CT9 19 H1
eens Gate Rd 11 24 D3
eens Gdns, Broadstairs 10 5 C5
eens Gdns, Herne Bay 6 12 C2
eens Gdns, Margate 9 19 H1
eens Prom CT9 20 A2
eens Rd, oadstairs CT10 5 B4
eens Rd, Canterbury 3 27 C1
eens Rd, Ramsgate 11 25 G3
eens Rd, estgate-on-Sea 8 18 B4
eens Rd, Whitstable 5 9 G2
eensbridge Dr 6 11 H1
erns Pl CT1 35 H2
erns Rd CT1 35 H2
etta Rd CT12 24 B1
ex Ct CT7 17 E4
ex Rd CT8 18 B5
ex View Rd CT7 16 D5

dley Cl CT10 23 G2
dnor Cl CT6 12 D5
glan Pl CT10 5 C3
lway Av CT5 9 F3
lway Ter CT9 3 B4
msey Cl CT2 35 E1
msey Ho CT1 6 A5
msgate Rd, Broadstairs T10 5 A5
nsgate Rd, Margate T9 19 G4
msgate Rd, Sandwich T13 29 F1
ncorn Rd CT9 18 D3
ndolph Cl CT1 35 G3
ndolph Ct CT8 17 H1
ndolph Ho CT9 3 E1
ndolph Sq CT9 3 F1
nelagh Gro CT10 23 E3
nsome Way CT7 16 D5
ttington St CT4 39 C2
vensbourne Av T6 12 D4
venscourt Rd CT2 30 B5
wdon Rd CT11 24 C4
yham Rd CT5 9 H4
ymond Av CT1 35 G3
ad Ct CT8 18 A4
ading St CT10 21 E6
Reading Street Rd CT10 20 D5
Rectory Gdns CT5 10 C3
Rectory Rd CT10 5 C2
Reculver Av CT7 16 C3
Reculver Cl CT6 13 H1
Reculver Dr CT6 13 G1
Reculver Rd CT6 13 E3
Reculvers Rd CT8 18 A5
Red Lion La*, Sea St CT5 9 E2
Redcot La CT2 33 F1
Redhill Rd CT8 17 H3
Redwood Cl, Canterbury CT2 31 E6
Redwood Cl, Chartham CT4 39 D3
Reed Av CT1 32 A5
Reeds Cl CT6 13 E2
Reeves Cl CT2 34 C2
Reeves Way CT5 10 B5
Regency Cl CT5 9 G4
Regency Ct CT11 4 B4
Regency Pl CT1 31 H6
Regent Dr CT6 13 E4
Regent St CT5 9 E2
Regents Walk CT6 13 F2
Reliance Dr CT6 13 E4
Remston Mews*, Military Rd CT1 31 H6
Renault Cl CT6 11 F2
Rentain Rd CT4 39 C2
Repton Cl CT10 23 E2
Reservoir Rd CT5 9 F1
Reynolds Cl CT6 12 D2
Rheims Ct CT2 34 D1
Rheims Way CT1 6 A4
Rhodaus Cl CT1 6 B5
Rhodaus Ho CT1 6 C6
Rhodaus Town CT1 6 B5
Rhodes Gdns CT10 23 F2
Richard Ct CT9 20 B3
Richardson Way CT12 26 B5
Richborough Rd, Sandwich CT13 29 E1
Richborough Rd, Westgate-on-Sea CT8 18 A5
Richmond Av CT9 20 A4
Richmond Ct CT6 12 B2
Richmond Dr CT6 13 H2
Richmond Gdns CT2 30 D6
Richmond Rd, Ramsgate CT11 4 B2
Richmond Rd, Whitstable CT5 10 A5
Richmond St CT6 12 B1
Ridgeway CT5 10 A5
Ridgeway Cliff CT6 11 H1
Ridgeway Rd CT6 14 C2
Ridgeway Walk CT6 14 D2
Riding Gate Pl CT1 6 C4
Ridley Cl CT6 12 C6
Rigby Ct CT1 31 H5
Riley Av CT6 11 E2
Riley Ter CT6 12 C5
Ringold Av CT12 24 B2
Ringsloe Ct CT7 16 B2
Ringwood Cl CT2 31 E5
Ripple Ct CT1 31 H6
Risdon Cl CT2 32 D1
River Bend Cl CT2 31 G6
River Ct CT4 39 B1
River Vw CT2 32 D1
Riverdale Rd CT1 31 H5
Riverdance Dr CT2 31 G6
Riverhead Cl CT9 20 B4
Rivers Ct CT12 15 C6
Riversdale Rd CT12 24 C1
Riverside CT4 39 B1
Riverside Cl CT4 37 B5
Riverside Cotts CT3 38 C1
Riverside Ct CT2 6 B2
Riverside Mews CT4 37 B5
Riverside Retail Pk CT1 34 D3
Roberts Rd CT5 8 B6
Robin Ct CT5 9 H1
Robin Ter CT1 6 D2
Rochester Av CT1 35 H3
Rochester Ct CT1 35 H4
Rockingham Pl CT6 13 E5
Rockstone Way CT12 24 B1
Rodney St CT11 4 B3
Roman Rd CT12 22 B6
Roman Row CT1 6 B4
Romilly Gdns CT12 22 C6
Romney Cl CT7 17 E4
Rope Walk Ho CT9 3 D3
Rope Walk Mews CT13 29 E2
Roper Cl CT2 6 A1
Roper Ho CT2 35 E1
Roper Rd CT2 6 A2
Rose Acre Rd CT3 38 A3
Rose Gdns, Birchington CT7 16 D5
Rose Gdns, Herne Bay CT6 13 E2
Rose Gdns, Ramsgate CT12 15 B5
Rose Hill CT11 4 C2
Rose La CT1 6 C4
Rose Sq CT1 6 C4
Rose Ter CT11 24 D4
Roseacre Cl CT2 35 E1
Roseacre Ct CT9 20 D3
Rosebery Av, Herne Bay CT6 13 G2
Rosebery Av, Ramsgate CT11 25 G2
Rosedale Rd CT9 19 H3
Roselands Gdns CT2 30 D6
Roselawn Gdns CT9 18 C4
Roselea Av CT6 12 C4
Rosemary Av CT10 5 A6
Rosemary Gdns, Broadstairs CT10 23 F6
Rosemary Gdns, Whitstable CT5 9 H4
Rosemary La CT1 6 A4
Rosetower Ct CT10 21 E5
Rosewood Way CT7 17 F3
Rosiers Ct CT2 6 A2
Ross Gdns CT2 30 B5
Rossetti Ct CT7 16 D3
Rossetti Rd CT7 16 D3
Rossland Rd CT12 24 B2
Rothsay Ct CT11 25 G1
Rothsay Ct*, Argyll Dr CT11 25 G1
Rough Common Rd CT2 30 B6
Rowan Cl CT2 32 D2
Rowan Ct CT10 5 A2
Rowan Tree Pk CT5 8 C6
Rowe Cl CT9 19 G5
Rowena Rd CT8 17 H1
Rowland Cres CT6 13 G2
Rowland Dr CT6 11 G4
Roxburgh Rd CT8 18 A4
Royal Av CT5 7 C1
Royal Cl CT10 23 E4
Royal Cres, Margate CT9 3 A3
Royal Cres, Ramsgate CT11 4 B4
Royal Ct CT5 9 H1
Royal Esp, Margate CT9 18 B3
Royal Esp, Ramsgate CT11 4 A4
Royal Harbour App CT11 24 C6
Royal Native Way CT5 8 C6
Royal Par CT11 25 F5
Royal Rd CT11 4 B3
Rugby Cl CT10 23 E3
Rumfields Rd CT10 22 C4
Runcie Ho CT1 6 A5
Runcie Pl CT2 34 D1
Runcie Pl*, Bishops Way CT2 34 D1
Rushmead Cl CT2 31 E6
Ruskins Vw CT6 12 D6
Russell Dr CT5 10 C3
Russett Cl CT13 27 D2
Russett Rd CT1 36 A3
Rutland Av CT9 20 B3
Rutland Cl CT1 36 B3
Rutland Gdns, Birchington CT7 16 D3
Rutland Gdns, Margate CT9 20 B3
Rydal Av CT11 24 B4
Ryde St CT2 35 E1
Ryders Av CT8 17 H2
Rye Walk CT6 13 F5

Sacketts Gap CT9 20 C2
Sacketts Hill CT10 22 B2
Saddlers Mews, Whitstable CT5 10 C4
Saddlers Mews, Ramsgate CT12 24 A1
Saddleton Gro CT5 9 E4
Saddleton Rd CT5 9 E4
St Albans Rd CT3 38 B4
St Alphege Cl CT5 8 C5
St Alphege Ct CT5 9 E3
St Alphege La CT1 6 C2
St Andrews Cl, Canterbury CT1 6 A5
St Andrews Cl, Herne Bay CT6 12 C3
St Andrews Cl, Margate CT9 19 G5
St Andrews Cl, Whitstable CT5 9 F5
St Andrews Ho CT1 6 A5
St Andrews Lees CT13 29 F3
St Andrews Rd CT11 25 G2
St Annes Ct CT6 12 B2
St Annes Dr CT6 12 A3
St Annes Gdns CT9 19 G5
St Annes Rd CT5 9 G1
St Anthonys Way CT9 20 B4
St Augustines Av CT9 19 G5
St Augustines Bsns Pk CT5 10 D3
St Augustines Cres CT5 10 C3
St Augustines Ct CT6 12 C4
St Augustines Pk, Ramsgate CT11 24 D5
St Augustines Pk, Westgate-on-Sea CT8 18 A5
St Augustines Rd, Canterbury CT1 35 H3
St Augustines Rd, Ramsgate CT11 4 A4
St Barts Rd CT13 29 E3
St Benedicts Lawn CT11 4 A4
St Benets Rd CT8 18 A5
St Catherinea Ct CT11 25 F1
St Catherines Ct*, Argyll Dr CT11 25 G1
St Catherines Gro CT12 26 D2
St Christopher Cl CT9 20 C5
St Christophers Grn CT10 23 F3
St Christophers Mews CT11 25 E2
St Clements CT13 29 F2
St Clements Ct CT10 23 E3
St Clements Rd CT8 18 A3
St Crispins Rd CT8 18 A5
St Davids Cl, Birchington CT7 17 F3
St Davids Cl, Whitstable CT5 9 G4
St Davids Rd CT11 25 G2
St Dunstans Cl CT2 35 E1
St Dunstans Ct CT2 35 E1
St Dunstans Rd CT9 20 A4
St Dunstans St CT2 35 E1
St Dunstans Ter CT2 35 E1
St Edmunds Rd CT1 6 B4
St Francis Cl CT9 20 C5
St Georges CT5 9 F5
St Georges Av CT6 11 H2
St Georges La CT1 6 C5
St Georges Lees CT13 29 F2
St Georges Pl, Canterbury CT1 6 D4
St Georges Pl, Sandwich CT13 29 G2
St Georges Rd, Broadstairs CT10 5 A4
St Georges Rd, Ramsgate CT11 25 G2
St Georges Rd, Sandwich CT13 29 F3
St Georges St CT1 6 C4
St Georges Ter CT6 12 A2
St Georges Ter*, St Georges La CT1 6 C5
St Gregorys Rd CT1 35 H1
St Jacobs Pl CT1 35 E4
St James Av, Broadstairs CT10 23 E3
St James Av, Ramsgate CT12 24 C1
St James Gdns CT5 9 E4
St James Park Rd CT9 18 B4
St James Ter CT7 17 F2
St Jeans Rd CT8 18 A6
St Johns Av East CT12 24 B1
St Johns Av West CT12 24 A1
St Johns Cres CT2 31 E1
St Johns Hospital CT1 6 D1
St Johns La CT1 6 B4
St Johns Pl CT1 6 D1
St Johns Rd, Margate CT9 3 D3
St Johns Rd, Whitstable CT5 10 C3
St Johns St CT9 3 D3
St Julien Av CT1 36 B1
St Lawrence CT11 24 D3
St Lawrence Av CT11 24 C6
St Lawrence Chase CT11 24 C4
St Lawrence Cl CT1 35 H3
St Lawrence Forstal CT1 35 H4
St Lawrence Ind Est CT11 24 C3
St Lawrence Rd CT1 35 H4
St Louis Gro CT6 11 H1
St Lukes Av CT11 25 E2
St Lukes Cl, Westgate-on-Sea CT8 18 A5
St Lukes Cl, Whitstable CT5 9 F5
St Lukes Rd CT11 25 F3
St Magnus Cl CT7 16 D2
St Magnus Ct*, St Magnus Cl CT7 17 E2
St Margarets Cl CT5 8 B6
St Margarets Rd CT8 18 A5
St Margarets St CT1 6 B4
St Marks Cl CT5 9 F4
St Martins Av CT1 35 H2
St Martins Cl CT1 35 H2
St Martins Hill CT1 36 A2
St Martins Hospital CT1 36 B2
St Martins Pl CT1 35 H2
St Martins Rd CT1 35 H2
St Martins Ter CT1 35 H2
St Martins Vw CT6 12 D6
St Marys Av CT9 20 C4
St Marys Cl, Eastry CT13 27 C5
St Marys Cl, Woodnesborough CT13 28 A5
St Marys Ct, Canterbury CT1 6 A4
St Marys Ct, Herne Bay CT6 12 B3
St Marys Gate CT13 29 F1
St Marys Gro CT5 8 A6
St Marys Rd, Broadstairs CT10 5 C3
St Marys Rd, Canterbury CT4 37 C3
St Marys Rd, Ramsgate CT12 15 B5
St Marys St CT1 6 B4
St Mawes CT8 18 A3
St Michaels Alley CT11 4 C2
St Michaels Av CT9 20 C5
St Michaels Cl CT2 30 B6
St Michaels Pl CT2 31 E6
St Michaels Rd CT2 31 E5
St Mildreds Av, Birchington CT7 16 C3
St Mildreds Av, Broadstairs CT10 5 A4
St Mildreds Av, Ramsgate CT11 24 D6
St Mildreds Ct, Westgate-on-Sea CT8 18 A3
St Mildreds Ct, Canterbury CT1 6 A3
St Mildreds Ct*, St Peters Pl CT1 6 A3
St Mildreds Gdns CT8 18 B3
St Mildreds Pl CT1 35 E3

St Mildreds Rd, Margate CT9 20 A4
St Mildreds Rd, Minster CT12 15 B6
St Mildreds Rd, Ramsgate CT11 24 D5
St Mildreds Rd, Westgate-on-Sea CT8 18 A4
St Nicholas Cl CT2 32 D1
St Nicholas Ct CT7 14 A5
St Nicholas Ho CT3 27 C2
St Nicholas Hospital CT2 34 C1
St Nicholas Rd CT1 34 D4
St Patricks Cl CT5 9 F5
St Patricks Rd CT11 25 G2
St Pauls Mews CT9 19 H2
St Pauls Rd CT9 19 H2
St Pauls Ter CT1 6 D4
St Peters Ct CT10 23 F3
St Peters Footpath CT9 3 E4
St Peters Gro CT1 6 A3
St Peters La CT1 6 B3
St Peters Park Rd CT10 5 A1
St Peters Pl CT1 6 A3
St Peters Rd, Broadstairs CT10 5 A3
St Peters Rd, Margate CT9 3 E4
St Peters St, Canterbury CT1 6 B2
St Peters St, Sandwich CT13 29 F1
St Peters St, Whitstable CT5 9 E2
St Radigunds Pl CT1 6 C1
St Saviours Ct CT8 18 A4
St Stephens Cl CT2 31 F6
St Stephens Ct CT2 31 F6
St Stephens Fld CT2 6 B1
St Stephens Footpath CT2 31 F6
St Stephens Grn CT2 31 F5
St Stephens Hill CT2 31 E3
St Stephens Manor CT10 21 G6
St Stephens Rd CT2 6 B1
St Swithins Rd CT5 10 A4
St Thomas Hill CT2 30 C5
St Vincents Cl, Canterbury CT3 38 A1
St Vincents Cl, Whitstable CT5 9 F5
Salisbury Av, Broadstairs CT10 23 F5
Salisbury Av, Ramsgate CT11 25 F3
Salisbury Rd, Canterbury CT2 31 E5
Salisbury Rd, Herne Bay CT6 13 E2
Salisbury Rd, Whitstable CT5 9 E4
Salmestone Rd CT9 19 G5
Salt Marsh La CT5 9 E2
Salts Cl CT5 9 E3
Salts Dr CT10 23 E3
Saltway Ct CT5 9 E4
Saltwood Gdns CT9 20 D3
San Remo CT8 18 A3
Sancroft Av CT2 34 D1
Sanctuary Cl CT10 23 F6
Sandalwood Dr CT7 14 C6
Sandend CT5 8 D6
Sanderling Rd CT6 13 H2
Sandhurst Cl CT2 31 G4
Sandhurst Rd CT9 21 E3
Sandles Rd CT7 16 D3
Sandown Dr CT6 12 A2
Sandown Lees CT13 29 H3
Sandown Rd CT13 29 F2
Sandpiper Ct*, Gainsboro Rd CT7 16 D2
Sandpiper Rd CT5 8 C6
Sandwich By-Pass CT13 28 C2
Sandwich Ind Est CT13 29 G1
Sandwich Rd, Canterbury CT3 27 C2
Sandwich Rd,Eastry CT13 27 C5
Sandwich Rd, Ramsgate CT12 26 C6
Sandwich Rd, Sandwich CT13 28 A1
Sandwich Rd, Woodnesborough CT13 28 C4
Sandwood Rd, Ramsgate CT11 25 G1
Sandwood Rd, Sandwich CT13 29 E2
Sanger Cl CT9 19 F4
Sangro Pl CT1 36 B1
Sarah Gdns CT9 20 C5
Sarre Pl CT13 29 E3
Saunders La CT3 27 D3
Savernake Dr CT6 12 D5
Saxon Pl CT6 12 C1
Saxon Rd, Canterbury CT4 37 B5
Saxon Rd, Ramsgate CT11 24 C5
Saxon Rd, Westgate-on-Sea CT8 18 B4
Saxon Shore CT5 8 D3
Sceales Dr CT12 26 B5
Sceptre Way CT5 8 D5
School La, Blean CT2 30 A1
School La, Fordwich CT2 33 E4
School La, Herne Bay CT6 12 D6
School La, Ickham CT3 38 D2
School La, Patrixbourne CT4 37 D1
School La, Ramsgate CT11 4 D1
School Path CT3 38 A3
School Rd, Canterbury CT3 27 B2
School Rd, Sandwich CT13 29 E1
Scott Av CT1 35 E4
Sea App CT10 5 C3
Sea Ct CT9 3 F1
Sea Point CT7 16 B2
Sea Rd CT7,8 17 F2
Sea St, Herne Bay CT6 11 G2
Sea St, Whitstable CT5 9 E2
Sea View Av CT7 16 C2
Sea View Heights CT7 16 B2
Sea View Rd, Birchington CT7 16 C2
Sea View Rd, Broadstairs CT10 23 G2
Sea View Rd, Herne Bay CT6 13 E1
Sea View Rd, Ramsgate CT12 26 C5
Sea View Sq CT6 12 B1
Sea View Ter CT9 19 E3
Sea Wall CT5 9 E2
Seacroft Rd CT10 25 H1
Seafield Rd, Broadstairs CT10 5 A4
Seafield Rd, Ramsgate CT11 24 D4
Seafield Rd, Whitstable CT5 10 A3
Seamark Rd CT7 16 C6
Seapoint Rd CT10 5 C5
Seasalter Beach CT5 8 C5
Seasalter La CT5 7 A2
Seaview Ct CT10 5 C5
Seaville Dr CT6 13 G1
Second Av, Broadstairs CT10 21 F3
Second Av, Margate C T9 20 A2
Seeshill Cl CT5 9 F4
Selbey Cl CT6 13 F3
Selborne Rd CT9 20 A5
Selsea Av CT6 11 H1
Selson La CT13 27 B5
Selwood Cotts CT6 13 F4
Selwyn Dr CT10 23 E3
Semaphore Rd CT7 16 D3
Semple Cl CT12 15 B4
Senlac Cl CT11 24 C5
Serene Ct CT10 5 C4
Setterfield Rd CT9 19 G4
Sevastopol Pl CT1 36 B1
Seven Posts Alley*, St Peters St CT13 29 F2
Seven Stones Dr CT10 25 H2
Sewell Cl CT7 17 E4
Seymour Av, Margate CT9 18 B4
Seymour Av, Whitstable CT5 9 F3
Seymour Cl CT6 12 D6
Seymour Pl CT1 35 E3
Shaftesbury Rd, Canterbury CT2 31 F5
Shaftesbury Rd, Hersden CT3 38 B5
Shaftesbury Rd, Whitstable CT5 9 E3
Shaftsbury St CT11 4 E1
Shah Pl*, Station Approach Rd CT11 25 E3
Shakespeare Pass CT9 3 A3
Shakespeare Rd, Birchington CT7 16 D2
Shakespeare Rd, Margate CT9 3 E4
Shalloak Rd CT2 32 B3
Shallows Rd CT10 22 C2
Shalmsford Ct CT4 39 A3
Shalmsford St CT4 39 A2
Shamrock Av CT5 8 C5
Shamrock Villas CT7 16 D5
Shapland Cl CT6 13 E3
Share and Coulter Rd CT5 10 C4
Shearwater Av CT5 8 D5
Sheehan Ho CT1 35 F4
Sheen Ct CT9 3 D4
Shelley Av CT1 32 A6
Shepherds Walk CT5 10 B6
Shepherds Way CT5 10 B6
Shepherdsgate CT2 6 A1
Shepherdsgate Dr CT6 14 C1
Sheppey Cl CT7 16 D4
Sheppey Vw CT5 8 D6
Sherwood Cl, Herne Bay CT6 13 E5
Sherwood Cl, Whitstable CT5 9 E6
Sherwood Dr CT5 8 D5
Sherwood Gdns CT11 25 F1
Sherwood Rd CT7 16 D5
Shipman Av CT2 34 C2
Shipwrights Lee CT5 9 E2
Shirley Av CT11 25 F1
Shore Cl CT6 11 G3
Short St CT13 29 F2
Shottendane Rd CT9 18 B6
Shuart La CT7 14 B5
Shutler Rd CT10 5 D3
Sidney Pl*, Market St CT9 3 D2
Silver Av CT7 17 E5
Silverdale Dr CT6 13 F5
Silverdale Rd CT11 24 B5
Simmonds Rd CT1 35 E3
Simon Av CT9 20 C3
Singer Av CT6 11 G2
Singleton Cl CT12 15 B6
Sion Ct CT11 4 C3
Sion Hill CT11 4 C3
Skinners Alley CT5 9 E2
Slades Cl CT5 10 B6
Sleigh Rd CT2 32 D2
Sloe La CT9 22 A3
Smugglers Way CT7 17 E2
Snell Gdns CT6 11 G4
Sobraon Way CT1 36 B1
Somerset Cl CT5 8 C5
Somerset Ct CT10 5 A3
Somerset Rd CT1 36 A2
Somme Ct CT1 36 B1
Somner Cl CT2 35 E1
Sondes Cl CT6 12 D5
South Canterbury Rd CT1 35 G4
South Cl CT1 6 C3
South Cliff Par CT10 25 H2
South Ct CT12 24 C1
South Eastern Rd CT11 4 A1
South Lodge CT5 9 F1
South Lodge Cl CT5 9 F1
South Rd CT6 12 C2
South St, Canterbury CT1 32 A5
South St, Whitstable CT5 9 H3
South View Rd CT5 9 E6
Southall Cl CT12 15 B4
Southover Ct CT11 4 F1
Southsea Dr CT6 12 A3
Southwold Pl CT8 17 H3
Southwood Gdns CT11 24 C4
Southwood Heights CT11 24 D4
Southwood Rd, Ramsgate CT11 24 D4
Southwood Rd, Whitstable CT5 10 A4
Sowell St CT10 23 F3
Spa Esp CT6 11 G1
Sparrow Castle CT9 3 E4
Sparrow Way CT3 38 D4
Speakman Ct CT11 24 D5
Speedwell Rd CT5 8 C6
Speke Rd CT10 23 E2
Speldhurst Gdns CT9 21 E2
Spencer Rd CT7 16 D2
Spencer Sq CT11 4 B4
Spencer St CT11 4 C3
Spenser Rd CT6 12 B3
Spicers Field CT6 13 F4
Spire Av CT5 9 H4
Spratling La CT12 24 A1
Spratling St CT12 24 A1
Spring Cl CT6 13 E2
Spring Gdns CT1 6 A6
Spring La, Canterbury CT1 35 H2
Spring La, Fordwich CT2 32 D4
Spring Walk CT5 9 E5
Springfield Cl, Broadstairs CT10 23 E6
Springfield Cl, Ramsgate CT11 25 F1
Springfield Rd CT9 20 D2
Squire Av CT2 34 D2
St Johns Pl CT5 10 C3
Staffordshire St CT11 4 D1
Staines Hill CT2 33 E1
Staines Pl, Broadstairs CT10 5 C2
Staines Pl, Canterbury CT1 6 C4
Stancomb Av CT11 24 D5
Standard Av CT6 11 F2
Staner Ct CT12 24 B3
Stanley Gdns CT6 12 C3
Stanley Pl, Broadstairs CT10 5 B3
Stanley Pl, Ramsgate CT11 25 E3
Stanley Rd, Broadstairs CT10 23 F2
Stanley Rd, Herne Bay CT6 12 C3
Stanley Rd, Margate CT9 19 H2
Stanley Rd, Ramsgate CT11 25 E3
Stanley Rd, Whitstable CT5 9 E4
Stanley Sykes Cl CT9 20 A5
Stanmore Ct CT1 35 H3
Staplehurst Av CT10 23 G6
Staplehurst Gdns CT9 21 E3
Star La CT9 22 A3
Starle Cl CT1 31 G6
Statenborough La CT13 27 B4
Station App, Birchington CT7 16 D3
Station App, Margate CT9 3 B3
Station App, Ramsgate CT12 15 B6
Station Approach Rd CT11 24 D2
Station Chine CT6 12 B3
Station Mews CT12 24 D2
Station Rd, Birchington CT7 16 D3
Station Rd, Bridge CT4 37 A5
Station Rd, Herne Bay CT6 12 B2
Station Rd, Margate CT9 3 A3
Station Rd, Patrixbourne CT4 37 C2
Station Rd, Ramsgate CT12 15 B6
Station Rd, Westgate-on-Sea CT8 18 A4
Station Rd, Whitstable CT5 9
Station Rd West CT2 6
Station Rd East CT1 6
Steed Cl CT6 14
Steeple Vw CT11 4
Stephen Cl CT10 5
Stephens Cl, Margate CT9 18
Stephens Cl, Ramsgate CT12 24
Stephenson Rd CT2 31
Sterling Cl CT10 23
Sterling Ct CT1 6
Steven Ct CT11 24
Stimson Ho CT9 19
Stirling Way CT12 24
Stock Ct CT2 30
Stockbury Gdns CT9 20
Stockwood Chase CT2 30
Stodmarsh Rd CT3 33
Stonar Cl, Ramsgate CT11 25
Stonar Cl, Sandwich CT13 29
Stonar Gdns CT13 29
Stonar Rd CT13 29
Stone Barn Av CT7 17
Stone Bay Ct CT10 5
Stone Cross Lees CT13 29
Stone Gdns CT10 5
Stone House Mews CT10 23
Stone Rd CT10 5
Stone Way CT3 38
Stonebridge Rd CT2 31
Stonerock Cl CT2 33
Stour Cl CT4 39
Stour Cres CT1 32
Stour Ct, Sandwich CT13 29
Stour Ct, Canterbury CT1 6
Stour Promenade CT1 31
Stour Rd CT4 39
Stour St CT1 6
Stour Villas CT1 6
Stourside Studios CT1 6
Strand St CT13 29
Strangers Cl CT1 34
Strangers La CT1 34
Strangford Pl CT6 13
Strangford Rd CT5 9
Strasbourg St CT9 22
Stream Walk CT5 9
Streete Court Rd CT8 18
Streete Ct CT8 18
Streetfield CT6 12
Stringer Dr CT7 17
Strode Park Rd CT6 12
Stuart Ct CT1 35
Studds Cotts CT6 11
Stuppington Court Fm CT1 35
Stuppington La CT1 35
Sturmer Cl CT1 36
Sturry Ct Mews CT2 32
Sturry Hill CT2 32
Sturry Rd CT1,2 31
Sudbury Pl CT8 17
Suffolk Av CT8 17
Suffolk Ct CT10 23
Suffolk Rd CT1 36
Suffolk St CT5 9
Sullivan Cl CT1 34
Summer Ct, Canterbury CT2 34
Summer Ct, Whitstable CT5 10
Summer Hill CT2 34
Summer La CT2 31
Summer Rd CT7 14
Summerfield Av CT5 9
Summerfield Rd CT9 21
Sun La CT7 14
Sun St CT1 6
Sunbeam Av CT6 11
Sundew Gro CT11 25
Sundridge Cl CT2 31
Sunningdale Walk CT6 11
Sunnyhill Rd CT6 11
Sunnymead CT2 30

nyside Gdns
13 28 D3
nyside Rd CT5 7 D1
ray Av CT5 8 C5
set Cl CT5 8 D6
rey Cl CT12 24 C1
rey Gdns CT7 16 D3
rey Rd, Canterbury
1 36 B3
rey Rd, Margate
9 20 B2
sex Av, Canterbury
1 36 A3
sex Av, Margate
9 19 G4
sex Cl CT6 11 G2
sex Gdns, Birchington
7 16 D3
sex Gdns, Herne Bay
6 11 G2
sex Gdns,
estgate-on-Sea
8 18 A3
sex Mansions
8 18 A3
sex St CT11 25 F3
herland Dr CT7 17 E4
ton Rd CT3 38 B4
akeley Walk CT5 10 B3
ale Cl CT6 12 D4
alecliffe Av CT6 11 F2
alecliffe Court Dr
5 10 C3
alecliffe Rd CT5 10 A4
allow Av CT5 8 D5
allow Cl CT9 19 E4
allow Ct CT6 14 B2
anfield Rd CT5 9 E3
anton La CT3 33 G6
aynes Way CT13 27 B6
eechbridge Rd
6 13 H3
eyn Rd CT9 19 H2
nburne Av CT10 5 A5
nford Gdns CT9 20 C5
amore Cl, Broadstairs
10 22 C4
amore Cl, Herne Bay
6 13 F2
amore Cl, Margate
9 19 F5
amore Grange
11 25 F1
enham St CT5 9 E2
ney Cooper Cl
2 30 B6
ney Rd, Ramsgate
11 25 G3
ney Rd, Whitstable
5 9 F4
dale Pl CT11 25 G3

dy Gdns CT9 20 C5
vera Rd CT1 36 A1
ot Av CT6 11 F2
ot Rd CT9 20 A4
head Rd CT6 12 D4
kerton Ct CT5 10 A3
kerton Heights
5 9 F1
kerton Mews CT5 9 F1
kerton Rd CT5 9 F1
nery La CT13 29 E2
nery Mws CT1 6 B4
nery Sq CT1 6 A4
nery Way North
1 6 A4
nery Way South
1 6 A4
lin Ct CT7 17 E3
sells Walk CT5 10 C3
istock Rd CT11 25 E1
lor Rd CT12 15 B5
Dr CT6 12 A4
dington Cl CT1 31 H6
egraph Hill Ind Est
12 15 C4
ord Ct CT6 11 H4
ord St CT6 12 B1
ham Av CT12 24 C3
nplars Ct CT2 6 A2
nple Ct CT2 34 D1
nple Mws CT1 6 B4
nple Rd CT2 34 D1
nple Way CT14 29 F6
Perch Rd CT1 34 D4
nyson Av CT1 32 A5
nyson Pl CT1 32 B5
terden Dr CT2 31 F4
Tenterden Way CT9 20 B5
Terminus Dr CT6 13 F2
Terrys La CT5 9 E2
Teynham Cl CT9 21 E3
Teynham Dr CT5 9 G2
Teynham Rd CT5 9 G2
Thanet Cl CT10 5 C2
Thanet Enterprise Centre
CT10 22 D1
Thanet Place Gdns
CT10 23 H2
Thanet Rd, Broadstairs
CT10 5 C3
Thanet Rd, Margate
CT9 3 E3
Thanet Rd, Ramsgate
CT11 25 G3
Thanet Rd, Westgate-on-Sea
CT8 17 H2
Thanet Reach Bsns Pk
CT10 22 B4
Thanet Vw CT7 14 C6
Thanet Way, Birchington
CT7 14 A4
Thanet Way, Herne Bay CT6
11 E3
Thanet Way, Whitstable
CT5 7 A3
Thanington Rd CT1 34 C4
The Avenue, Hersden
CT3 38 A5
The Avenue,
Margate CT9 19 H3
The Banks CT10 23 F2
The Barges CT5 9 F1
The Borough CT1 6 C2
The Boundary CT1 34 D4
The Briars CT5 8 D6
The Bridge App CT5 9 G2
The Broadway, Broadstairs
CT10 5 A3
The Broadway, Herne Bay
CT6 11 G1
The Broadway, Ramsgate
CT11 4 B3
The Bungalows
CT13 28 A5
The Butchery*, Market St
CT13 29 F1
The Butts CT13 29 E1
The Causeway, Canterbury
CT2 6 B1
The Causeway, Sandwich
CT13 28 C1
The Cedars CT1 6 A5
The Centre CT9 3 D3
The Chain CT13 29 F2
The Chalet CT5 7 B1
The Chase, Ramsgate
CT11 25 G2
The Chase, Whitstable
CT5 8 D4
The Chaucer Bsns Pk
CT5 7 C1
The Circus CT6 12 A3
The City Gdns CT1 6 C4
The Cloisters CT11 4 B4
The Close, Bridge
CT4 37 A5
The Close, Canterbury
CT2 31 F4
The Close, Rough Common
CT2 30 C5
The Close*, Cockering Rd
CT1 34 D4
The Coppice CT2 32 D2
The Courts CT9 18 B4
The Courtyard CT12 26 C2
The Crescent, Canterbury
CT2 31 F4
The Crescent, Chartham
CT4 39 C3
The Crescent, Sandwich
CT13 28 D5
The Crescent, Whitstable
CT5 10 A5
The Cross CT13 27 C6
The Cuttings CT12 24 D2
The Dene CT1 35 H5
The Downings CT6 12 D4
The Downs, Canterbury
CT4 39 C3
The Downs, Ramsgate
CT11 4 A4
The Drive, Canterbury
CT1 35 H4
The Drive, Whitstable
CT5 10 C5
The Drove, Canterbury CT2
32 D4
The Drove, Whitstable
CT5 10 C6
The Elders CT3 38 A1
The Elms CT3 38 B5
The Exchange CT5 9 G1
The Fairway CT6 12 A5
The Finches CT7 14 B5
The Firs CT3 38 B5
The Footpath CT10 5 C3
The Foreland CT1 35 H5
The Frank Walters Bsns Pk
CT10 22 D4
The Friars CT1 6 B3
The Gables Villas CT11 4 A1
The Gap, Blean CT2 30 A1
The Gap, Canterbury
CT1 35 H5
The Grange, Whitstable
CT5 8 B6
The Grange, Ramsgate
CT11 24 D5
The Green, Blean CT2 30 A2
The Green, Chartham
CT4 39 C1
The Green, Littlebourne
CT3 38 B3
The Green, Ramsgate
CT12 26 D2
The Grove, Herne Bay
CT6 11 H4
The Grove, Westgate-on-Sea
CT8 18 A4
The Halt CT5 9 H5
The Hamele CT2 32 C3
The Hawthorns CT10 22 C4
The Heath CT5 10 A5
The Heights CT5 8 D5
The Hill CT3 38 A2
The Horshams CT6 13 G2
The Hoystings Cl
CT1 6 D6
The Hyde CT4 39 A2
The Knights Apts
CT1 35 H3
The Lancaster CT10 5 C5
The Lanes CT12 15 C5
The Larches CT5 9 E4
The Leas CT5 10 B5
The Lees CT6 13 E1
The Length CT7 14 B5
The Malthouses CT7 16 D3
The Maltings, Canterbury
CT2 6 A1
The Maltings, Littlebourne
CT3 38 B3
The Maltings, Ramsgate
CT11 4 B1
The Mansions CT10 23 E4
The Maples CT10 22 C4
The Meadows CT6 13 F4
The Merchant Store
CT2 6 A1
The Mews Apts CT1 35 H3
The Mint CT2 34 C1
The Ness CT1 35 G5
The New Cl CT4 37 B4
The Nook CT12 22 C5
The Oaks, Birchington
CT7 14 B5
The Oaks, Broadstairs
CT10 21 E6
The Oaks, Hersden
CT3 38 B5
The Oaks, Whitstable
CT5 8 C6
The Oaze CT5 8 D6
The Old Stables, Ramsgate
CT11 24 D5
The Old Stables, Margate
CT9 3 F2
The Orchard Residences
CT1 35 G5
The Oysters CT5 9 F1
The Paddock CT1 35 H2
The Paddocks, Broadstairs
CT10 21 F6
The Paddocks, Herne Bay
CT6 13 H2
The Paddocks, Margate
CT9 20 C4
The Parade, Birchington
CT7 16 B3
The Parade, Broadstairs
CT10 5 C3
The Parade, Canterbury
CT1 6 C3
The Parade, Margate
CT9 3 D2
The Parkway CT7 17 E4
The Passage CT9 3 F1
The Pathway CT10 5 C3
The Pines, Broadstairs
CT10 22 C4
The Pines, Canterbury
CT1 35 G4
The Poplars CT3 38 C5
The Promenade
CT10 23 H5
The Quay CT13 29 F2
The Quick CT3 27 C1
The Rendezvous CT9 3 D1
The Retreat, Birchington
CT7 17 E2
The Retreat, Ramsgate
CT12 24 C2
The Ridgeway, Broadstairs
CT10 23 E5
The Ridgeway, Margate
CT9 20 B4
The Ridings, Margate
CT9 20 D2
The Ridings, Whitstable
CT5 10 C5
The Rope Walk CT1 6 A4
The Russets CT5 10 C5
The Saltings CT5 9 E2
The Savoy CT11 4 A3
The School Cl CT8 17 H1
The Sidings CT5 9 F2
The Silvers CT10 22 C4
The Spinney CT9 20 D4
The Spires CT2 31 F6
The Square CT7 17 E4
The Street, Ash CT3 27 B2
The Street, Birchington
CT7 14 B5
The Street, Deal CT14 29 F6
The Street, Ickham
CT3 38 D1
The Street, Patrixbourne
CT4 37 C3
The Street, Sandwich
CT13 28 B4
The Street, Ramsgate
CT12 15 B1
The Sycamores CT3 38 B5
The Terrace CT2 31 F5
The Vale CT10 5 A4
The Vespers CT2 6 B1
The Villas CT3 38 C5
The Vines CT5 9 E2
The Warren CT5 9 E6
The Warren Dr CT8 17 G3
Third Av CT9 20 A2
Thirlmere Av CT11 24 B4
Thistle Dr CT5 8 C6
Thomas Way CT3 38 D5
Thorn Gdns CT11 25 F1
Thornden Cl CT6 11 F3
Thornden Ct CT2 30 C4
Thornden Wood Rd
CT6 11 F6
Thorne Rd CT12 15 B5
Thornhurst CT6 13 F2
Thornton La CT13 27 A6
Three Kings Alley*,
St Peters St CT13 29 F2
Three Kings Yard*,
St Peters St CT13 29 F2
Throwley Cotts CT9 18 C5
Throwley Dr CT6 11 H2
Thrupp Pad CT10 21 F4
Thruxted La CT4 39 A3
Thundersland Rd
CT6 12 D3
Thurlow Av CT6 13 E1
Thurston Pk CT5 9 F3
Tile Kiln Hill CT2 30 B3
Tina Gdns CT10 23 G2
Tippledore La CT10 23 E3
Tivoli Brooks CT9 19 F4
Tivoli Park Av CT9 3 B4
Tivoli Rd CT9 19 F5
Tollemache Cl CT12 26 A2
Tollgate Cl CT5 9 E4
Tomlin Dr CT9 20 C6
Tomsons Pass CT11 4 B1
Tonford La CT1 34 B4
Torrington Cotts
CT12 15 C5
Tothill St CT12 15 B5
Tourtel Rd CT1 31 G6
Tower Bungalows
CT7 17 E2
Tower Gdns CT6 12 B1
Tower Hill CT5 9 F1
Tower Par CT5 9 F1
Tower Rd CT5 9 F1
Tower Vw CT4 39 D3
Tower Way CT1 6 B3
Town Hill CT4 37 A4
Townley St CT11 4 B3
Tradewinds CT5 8 C6
Trafalgar Mews CT11 4 B3
Treasury Vw CT3 38 D2
Trenley Dr CT3 36 D1
Trilby Way CT5 8 D6
Trinity Ct, Margate
CT9 3 E1
Trinity Ct, Ramsgate
CT11 4 F1
Trinity Hill CT9 3 D2
Trinity Pl CT11 25 G3
Trinity Sq, Broadstairs
CT10 21 F6
Trinity Sq, Margate
CT9 3 E1
Trotwood Pl*, Albion St
CT10 5 C4
Troughton Mews
CT9 3 B4
Trove Ct CT11 4 E1
Trueman Cl CT2 30 A1
Truro Rd CT11 4 F1
Tudor Cl CT7 17 F3
Tudor Ct, Canterbury
CT2 30 C4
Tudor Ct, Whitstable
CT5 9 H1
Tudor Rd CT1 6 A6
Tunis Ct CT1 36 B1
Tunis Row CT10 5 C2
Tunstall Rd CT2 31 G4
Turnagain La CT1 6 C3
Turnden Gdns CT9 20 D3
Turner Ct CT9 19 H2
Turner Heights CT9 3 F2
Turner St CT11 4 D2
Twyne Cl CT2 32 D2
Tydemans Av CT5 10 B5
Tyler Cl CT2 31 F5
Tyler Hill Rd CT2 30 A2
Tyler Way CT5 10 D3
Tyndale Pk CT6 12 D2
Tyson Av CT9 18 B4

Ulcombe Gdns CT2 31 G4
Ulster Rd CT9 19 G4
Underdown La CT6 12 C4
Underdown Rd CT6 12 C2
Underwood Cl CT1 35 G5
Union Cres CT9 3 D3
Union Pl CT1 6 D1
Union Rd, Canterbury
CT4 37 A5
Union Rd, Ramsgate
CT11 25 G2
Union Row CT9 3 D2
Union Sq CT10 5 D3
Union St, Canterbury
CT1 6 D2
Union St, Ramsgate
CT11 4 D1
Unity Pl CT11 25 G3
University Rd CT2 30 D5
Upchurch Walk CT9 21 E4
Uplands CT2 31 F4
Upper Approach Rd
CT10 5 B5
Upper Bridge St CT1 6 C5
Upper Chantry La CT1 6 D5
Upper Dane Rd CT9 20 A4
Upper Dumpton Park Rd
CT11 25 F3
Upper Free Down
CT6 12 D4
Upper Gore La
CT13 27 A6
Upper Gro CT9 3 E3
Upper Maltings Pl
CT7 16 D3
Upper Strand St
CT13 29 F2
Upton Rd CT10 23 F3
Ursuline Dr CT8 17 G3

Vale Pl CT11 4 A2
Vale Rd, Broadstairs
CT10 23 E4
Vale Rd, Ramsgate
CT11 4 A2
Vale Rd, Whitstable
CT5 9 F4
Vale Sq CT11 4 A3

Valkyrie Av CT5 8 D4
Valley Rd, Broadstairs CT10 22 C1
Valley Rd, Canterbury CT1 35 E4
Vauxhall Av, Canterbury CT1 32 A4
Vauxhall Av, Herne Bay CT6 11 F2
Vauxhall Cres CT1 32 A4
Vauxhall Industrial Rd CT1 32 A4
Vauxhall Rd CT1 32 A4
Ventnor La CT9 3 E4
Vere Rd CT10 5 B3
Vereth Rd CT11 4 A3
Vernon Pl CT1 6 D5
Veronica Ct CT6 12 A2
Verwood Cl CT2 31 E5
Vesty Ct CT8 18 A3
Viaduct Cl CT12 24 D2
Vicarage Cres CT9 19 G4
Vicarage La, Canterbury CT2 30 B2
Vicarage La, Sandwich CT13 29 E1
Vicarage Pl CT9 3 D4
Vicarage St CT10 22 D3
Victor Av CT9 20 D3
Victoria Av, Broadstairs CT10 20 D6
Victoria Av, Margate CT9 20 A4
Victoria Av, Westgate-on-Sea CT8 18 A5
Victoria Ct CT9 19 E3
Victoria Dr CT6 11 H1
Victoria Ho, Westgate-on-Sea CT8 18 D4
Victoria Ho, Ramsgate CT11 4 E2
Victoria Mews CT8 18 B4
Victoria Par, Broadstairs CT10 5 C5
Victoria Par, Ramsgate CT11 4 F1
Victoria Pk CT6 12 C2
Victoria Pl CT8 17 H1
Victoria Rd, Broadstairs CT10 23 E2
Victoria Rd, Canterbury CT1 35 E3
Victoria Rd, Margate CT9 3 E4
Victoria Rd, Ramsgate CT11 4 F1
Victoria Row, Canterbury CT1 6 D2
Victoria Row, Ramsgate CT11 24 D5
Victoria St CT5 9 E2
Victoria Yd CT1 6 D2
Viking Cl CT7 16 B3
Viking Ct, Broadstairs CT10 5 C6
Viking Ct, Margate CT9 20 A2
Villiers Ho CT10 23 G1
Villiers Rd CT1 36 B1
Vincent Cl CT12 22 C5
Vine Cl CT11 22 D6
Vine Lodge*, Vine Cl CT12 23 E6
Vinten Cl CT6 14 D1
Violet Av CT12 22 C6
Virginia Rd CT5 9 H4
Viscount Cl CT6 12 D4
Vulcan Cl CT5 9 E4
Vyeson Ct CT11 4 C2

Wacher Cl CT2 31 F6
Wacher Ct CT6 12 C1
Wainwright Ct CT10 23 H2
Walcot Pl CT6 13 E4
Walden Ct CT2 31 G5
Waldron Rd CT10 23 G6
Walker La CT7 16 B2
Wallace Way CT10 23 E4
Wallis Ct CT6 13 H2
Wallwood Rd CT11 25 G2
Walmer Gdns CT12 26 B6
Walmer Rd CT5 9 F4
Walmsley Rd CT10 5 A2
Walnut Cl CT10 23 F6
Walnut Mews CT7 16 D3
Walnut Tree Cl CT7 17 E4
Walnut Tree La CT3 33 G1
Walpole Rd CT9 3 E2
Waltham Cl CT9 21 E3
Wantsum Cl CT6 13 H1
Wantsum Mews*, Loop St CT13 29 E1
Wantsum Way CT7 14 B5
Wantsume Lees CT13 28 D1
Wardour Cl CT10 5 C3
Warre Av CT11 24 D5
Warren Dr CT10 23 E3
Warten Rd CT11 25 G1
Warwick Dr CT11 24 C5
Warwick Rd, Canterbury CT1 36 A2
Warwick Rd, Margate CT9 20 B3
Warwick Rd, Whitstable CT5 9 E2
Watchester Av CT11 4 A4
Watchester La CT12 15 B6
Water La, Canterbury CT1 6 B4
Water La, Fordwich CT2 32 D3
Water Mdws CT2 32 D3
Waterloo Pl CT11 4 E1
Waterloo Rd CT5 9 E2
Waters Edge CT2 31 G5
Waterside Dr CT8 18 A3
Watling St CT1 6 B4
Watts Yd CT13 29 E2
Wauchope Rd CT5 8 B5
Wave Crest CT5 8 D3
Waverley Rd CT9 18 D4
Way Hill CT12 15 D5
Wayborough Hill CT12 15 D5
Wayfarer Cl CT6 12 D4
Wayne Cl CT10 23 E3
Wealdhurst Pk CT10 22 D3
Weatherly Dr CT10 23 F6
Weddington La CT3 27 C1
Weigall Pl CT11 24 C4
Weir Ct CT1 31 H6
Well Cl CT2 33 E1
Well La CT2 32 D4
Wellesley Cl, Broadstairs CT10 23 E5
Wellesley Cl, Westgate-on-Sea CT8 18 A6
Wellesley Ct CT11 4 D1
Wellesley Rd, Margate CT9 20 A4
Wellesley Rd, Westgate-on-Sea CT8 18 A5
Wellington Cres CT11 4 E2
Wellington Rd CT8 18 A5
Wellington St CT5 7 D1
Wellis Gdns CT9 19 E4
Wells Av CT1 35 H3
Welsdene Rd CT9 18 C5
Wemyss Way CT1 36 A1
Wentworth Av CT9 18 B4
Wentworth Dr CT12 24 B2
Wentworth Gdns CT6 12 A5
West Beach CT5 8 D3
West Cliff CT5 9 E3
West Cliff Av CT10 5 C5
West Cliff Dr CT6 11 G2
West Cliff Gdns CT6 11 G2
West Cliff Mws CT10 5 C5
West Cliff Prom CT11 4 A4
West Cliff Rd, Broadstairs CT10 5 B5
West Cliff Rd, Ramsgate CT11 4 A3
West Dumpton La CT11 25 F1
West Hill Rd CT6 11 H1
West Park Av CT9 20 C4
West Pl*, Roseacre Cl CT2 35 E1
West View Cl CT6 11 G4
Westbere La CT2 33 E1
Westbrook Av CT9 18 B4
Westbrook Cotts CT9 19 E3
Westbrook Gdns CT9 18 D3
Westbrook Ho CT8 18 D4
Westbrook La CT6 11 F3
Westbrook Prom CT9 18 B3
Westbrook Rd CT9 19 E3
Westbury Rd CT8 18 A4
Westcliff Gdns CT9 18 D3
Westcliff Arc*, Rose Hill CT11 4 C4
Westcliff Arcade CT11 4 D3
Westcliff Ct CT10 5 C5
Westcliff Rd CT9 18 D3
Westcliff Ter CT11 24 C5
Westerham Cl, Canterbury CT2 31 G4
Westerham Cl, Margate CT9 21 E4
Westerly Mews CT2 35 E1
Western Av, Canterbury CT4 37 B5
Western Av, Herne Bay CT6 12 A2
Western Esp, Broadstairs CT10 23 G6
Western Esp, Herne Bay CT6 11 G1
Western Rd CT9 20 B5
Western Undercliff CT11 24 C6
Westfield CT2 30 A1
Westfield Rd, Birchington CT7 16 D3
Westfield Rd, Margate CT9 18 D5
Westgate Bay Av CT8 17 H2
Westgate Cl CT2 34 C1
Westgate Court Av CT2 34 C1
Westgate Garden Flats CT1 6 A3
Westgate Gro CT2 6 A2
Westgate Hall Rd CT1 6 B2
Westgate Ter CT5 9 F2
Westlands Rd CT6 11 G3
Westleigh Rd CT8 17 G2
Westmarsh Dr CT9 21 E4
Westmeads Rd CT5 9 F1
Westminster Rd CT1 32 A4
Westminster Walk CT12 24 D2
Westmount Ho CT9 20 A2
Westonville Av CT9 18 C3
Westover Gdns CT10 23 E1
Westover Rd CT10 23 E1
Westside Apts CT2 6 A2
Westwood Cross Shopping Mall CT10 22 A4
Westwood Dr CT2 31 G6
Westwood Gateway CT9 22 A3
Westwood Ind Est CT9 22 A2
Westwood Rd CT10 22 B4
Westwood Retail Pk CT10 22 A3
Weyburn Dr CT12 24 B1
Wharfedale Rd CT9 19 H3
Whatmer Cl CT2 33 E1
Wheatley Pl CT9 3 E4
Wheatley Rd, Ramsgate CT12 24 D1
Wheatley Rd, Whitstable CT5 9 F2
Wheelwrights Way CT13 27 B6
Whinfell Av CT11 24 A3
Whitbourne Ct*, Essex Rd CT5 9 E4
White Hart Mansions CT9 3 D2
White Horse La CT1 6 B3
White Marsh Ct CT5 9 F2
White Post Gdns CT3 27 C2
White Wood Rd CT13 27 B6
Whitefriars Mdw CT13 29 E2
Whitefriars Shopping Centre CT1 6 C4
Whitefriars St CT1 6 C4
Whitefriars Way, Sandwich CT13 29 E2
Whitefriars Way, Canterbury CT1 6 C4
Whitehall Bridge Rd CT2 35 E1
Whitehall Cl CT2 35 E1
Whitehall Gdns CT2 6 A3
Whitehall Rd, Canterbury CT2 6 A3
Whitehall Rd, Ramsgate CT12 24 C2
Whiteness Grn CT10 21 E4
Whiteness Rd CT10 21 F4
Whitepost CT5 9 E2
Whitfield Av CT10 20 D6
Whitgift Ct CT2 34 D1
Whitstable & Tankerton Hosp CT5 9 H2
Whitstable Rd, Blean CT2 30 B4
Whitstable Rd, Canterbury CT2 31 E6
Whitstable Rd, Herne Bay CT6 11 E3
Whytecliffs Par CT10 23 G6
Wichling Cl CT2 31 G4
Wickets End CT5 9 E3
Wickham Av CT11 25 G2
Wickham La CT3 38 D1
Wife of Bath Hill CT2 34 C2
Wigwam Pad CT7 17 E2
Wilbrough Rd CT7 17 E3
Wild Air CT7 16 D2
Wilderness Hill CT9 3 F3
Wildwood Rd CT2 32 D2
Wilfred Rd CT11 24 D3
Wilkes Rd CT10 23 E5
Wilkie Rd CT7 17 E2
William Av CT9 20 C5
William St CT6 12 C2
Willow Av CT10 22 D4
Willow Cl, Canterbury CT2 31 G5
Willow Cl, Margate CT9 20 C4
Willow Ct, Broadstairs CT10 5 A2
Willow Ct, Whitstable CT5 9 F4
Willow Farm Way CT6 13 E4
Willow Mws CT6 12 C6
Willow Rd CT5 7 C1
Willow Tree Cl CT6 13 F2
Willow Way, Margate CT9 19 E4
Willow Way, Whitstable CT5 10 B5
Willowbank CT13 29 F1
Willowbrook Cl CT6 12 D4
Willows Ct CT2 30 C4
Willsons Rd CT11 4 A3
Wilmott Pl CT13 27 B5
Wilton Rd CT12 24 A2
Wimborne Pl CT12 24 C2
Wincheap CT1 6 A6
Wincheap Ind Est CT1 34 D3
Winchester Gdns CT1 35 G4
Windermere Av CT11 24 B4
Windmill Av CT12 22 B5
Windmill Cl, Bridge CT4 37 B5
Windmill Cl, Canterbury CT1 36 A2
Windmill Cl, Herne Bay CT6 12 D5
Windmill Ct CT5 9 E5
Windmill Rd, Canterbury CT1 36 A2
Windmill Rd, Herne Bay CT6 12 D5
Windmill Rd, Whitstable CT5 9 E5
Windmill Vw CT9 19 H4
Windmill Walk CT12 24 C1
Windsor Av CT9 20 A4
Windsor Cl CT10 23 E3
Windsor Ct CT9 20 A5
Windsor Ct*, Laleham Walk CT9 20 A5
Windsor Gdns CT6 11 G3
Windsor Ho CT5 9 F3
Windsor Mews CT9 3 D4
Windsor Rd, Canterbury CT1 34 C4
Windsor Rd, Ramsgate CT12 26 C4
Wingham Rd CT3 38 D2
Wings Cl CT10 5 D1
Winifred Av CT12 22 C6
Winkle Cl CT6 11 G3
Winstanley Cres CT11 2
Winston Cl CT1 3
Winston Ct CT7 1
Winston Gdns CT6 1
Winterstoke Cres CT11 25
Winterstoke Undercliff CT11 25
Winterstoke Way CT11 25
Wolseley Av CT6
Wood Hill CT2 3
Woodberry Flats CT10
Woodcote CT5 1
Woodford Av CT12 2
Woodford Ct CT7 1
Woodland Av CT7 1
Woodland Rd CT6 1
Woodland Way, Broadsta CT10 2
Woodland Way, Canterb CT2 3
Woodland Way, Sandwic CT13 2
Woodlawn St CT5
Woodman Av CT5 1
Woodnesborough La CT13 2
Woodnesborough Rd CT13 2
Woodrow Chase CT6 1
Woods Ley CT3 2
Woodside Av CT4 3
Woodside Rd CT2 3
Woodvale Av CT5 1
Woodville CT2 3
Woodville Cl CT1 3
Woodville Rd CT12 2
Woollets Cl CT6 1
Worcester Gro CT10 2
Worcester La CT3 3
Worthgate Pl CT1
Wotton Ct CT7 1
Wraik Hill CT5
Wrentham Av CT6
Wrotham Av CT10
Wrotham Rd CT10
Wye Gdns CT9 2
Wyndham Av CT9 2
Wynellis Ho CT5
Wynn Rd CT5

Yardhurst Gdns CT9 2
Yardley Ho CT10 2
Yarrow Cl CT10
Yeomans Dr CT2 3
Yew Tree Cl CT10 2
Yew Tree Cotts CT4 3
Yew Tree Ct CT3 3
Yew Tree Gdns, Birchingt CT7 1
Yew Tree Gdns, Canterbu CT2 3
Yoakley Ho CT9 1
Yoakley Sq CT9 1
York Av CT10
York Cl CT6 1
York Rd, Canterbury CT1
York Rd, Herne Bay CT6 1
York St, Broadstairs CT10
York St, Ramsgate CT11
York Ter CT7 1
Ypres Ct CT1 36

Zealand Rd CT1 3
Zion Pl CT9